CW00675994

Edgar Cayce's
A S T R O L O G Y
for the Soul

Edgar Cayce's
ASTROLOGY
for the Soul

Margaret Gammon
and
W.H. Church

ARE
PRESS

ASSOCIATION FOR
RESEARCH AND
ENLIGHTENMENT

A.R.E. Press • Virginia Beach • Virginia

Copyright © 1998
by the Association for
Research and Enlightenment, Inc.

1st Printing, October 1998

Printed in the U.S.A.

All rights reserved. No part of this book may be repro-
duced or transmitted in any form or by any means, electronic or mechanical, including photocopying, recording
or by any information storage and retrieval system, without permission in writing from the Publisher.

A.R.E. Press
215 67th Street
Virginia Beach, VA 23451-2061

Astrology and the Edgar Cayce Readings
© 1967, 1973 by the Edgar Cayce Foundation

Articles by W.H. Church reprinted from *Gods in the Making*
© 1983 by the Edgar Cayce Foundation

Library of Congress Cataloging-in-Publication Data
    Gammon, Margaret.
    Edgar Cayce's astrology for the soul / Margaret Gammon,
W.H. Church
        p.   cm.
    ISBN 0-87604-411-9 (trade paper)
    1. Astrology. 2. Cayce, Edgar, 1877-1945. Edgar Cayce read-
ings. I. Church, W. H. II. Title.
BF1711.G35   1998
1133.5—dc21   98-38842

Edgar Cayce readings © 1971, 1993, 1994, 1995, 1996
by the Edgar Cayce Foundation
All rights reserved.

Cover design by Lightbourne Images

Contents

Preface .... *vii*

Part 1

Foreword *1*

1 The Language of the Readings 6

2 Akasha: The Soul's Record of Evolutionary
Progress 14

3 The Great Plan of Soul Evolution 23

4 The Planets 37

5 Cusps and the Zodiac 72

6 Planets, Transits, and Cycles 88

Summary 98

*Appendix I: Birth Charts and Examples of Life
Readings* *101*

Appendix II: Zodiac—Planetary Signs and Symbols .. *113*

Glossary *119*

Part 2

The Music of the Spheres 129

Sunspots: Signs of Turmoil 165

Age of Glory 177

Notes *197*

Preface

Edgar Cayce, America's best-documented psychic, first became known for his psychic readings on medical problems. He helped many people heal themselves of a wide variety of ailments. Eventually, however, the scope of his psychic readings broadened to include many philosophical and spiritual subjects. Among the amazing information that flowed through Cayce were many references to astrology.

The Edgar Cayce material presented a unique approach to astrology—one that was first and foremost designed to help the specific individual for whom the psychic reading was given. Only occasionally were general questions asked of the Cayce source about astrology and its finer points of application—no uniform system of astrology was presented by the Cayce readings.

The two authors of this book have attempted through their research into both astrology and the Cayce material to synthesize and reveal an astrology that is useful, insightful, and, indeed, spiritually focused. Edgar Cayce himself would have had it no other way. For, he wanted no part of any philosophy that did not make a person a kinder, more loving individual—one who made the world a better place for having lived in it.

Edgar Cayce's Astrology for the Soul is presented in two parts. Margaret Gammon's original bestseller about Cayce's approach to astrology makes up the first part, and a fascinating selection of classic articles by W.H. Church on a new approach to astrology for these times comprises part two. Together this material presents an excellent overview of traditional astrology, how the readings view it and sometimes disagree with it, and how the two combine to form a more meaningful tool for greater self-understanding.

Part 1

Foreword

How Astrology Entered into the Readings

Prior to 1923 Edgar Cayce spent over twenty years giving physical readings without any mention or commentary on the subjects of astrology, philosophy, or metaphysics.

Then in Dayton, Ohio, a man named Arthur Lammers, who was interested in Cayce's work and who had devoted considerable study to philosophy and comparative religions, suggested some nonroutine questions be posed to the sleeping Cayce. The answers which came through proved a major surprise for the Cayce family and served as the basis for a new type of clairvoyant discourse—the life reading. A more detailed story of this is related in the biography *There Is a River*, by Thomas Sugrue.

It should be noted that Cayce was throughout his lifetime a devout Christian and a Sunday school teacher. He had no background whatever in astrology or religious philosophy beyond his own fundamental biblical beliefs.

Consequently, the comments which came through the life readings on such subjects as planetary sojourns, akashic records, and past incarnations were decidedly alien to the waking Cayce's manner of thinking. Nevertheless, the life readings were pursued from 1923 onward and comprise a major portion of the material in the Cayce files.

Any study of the life readings provides the reader with numerous references to planetary and astrological influences. How these compare with traditional concepts of astrology will rest largely upon the reader's own background and knowledge on the subject.

It should be noted from the beginning, however, that traditional astrological thought maintains that "the stars incline—they do not compel." And this view was fully reiterated by Cayce:

> *But let it be understood here, no action of any planet or the phases of the sun, the moon or any of the heavenly bodies surpass the rule of man's will power* . . . The inclinations of man are ruled by the planets under which he is born, for the destiny of man lies within the sphere or scope of the planets. 3744-4

Or, as he stated again and again, "Mind is ever the builder."

What, then, are the planetary influences? What should the study of astrology be concerned with? And if we are not compelled, how are we inclined by our planetary relationships?

To understand fully the complexities of traditional astrology requires considerable study and years of carefully applied experience. Consequently, no complete summary of that subject in comparison with the life readings will be accomplished by this brief text, which can serve only as a springboard to additional research in the combined fields.

With this in mind, our hope is that students of parapsychology and astrologers alike may approach the body of information within the readings with open minds, since there are questions that arise which are not easily resolved.

The major variance, or addition, as it exists within the readings, is based upon the concept of reincarnation and its relationship to various planetary influences. These influences are indicated to be the result of planetary relationships developed during or between previous lives. In fact, of the nearly 2,000 life readings which Cayce gave from 1923 to 1945, almost all refer to past incarnations and specific astrological or planetary influences bearing upon the present.

Past earth experiences, according to the readings, express themselves through an individual's emotions—while at the same time individuals' mental aspects are shown as being developed from dwelling in planes of consciousness (represented by planets) between earth lives. Planetary relationships are thus explained as being symbolic of these experiences and the development achieved. Consequently, each individual varies considerably not only in mental and emotional traits, but also in the manner or degree that a given planet or planetary configuration affects that person.

In brief, planetary relationships are explained as being part of a great plan for soul development, which will be covered in more detail in the following chapters. This plan calls for the individual soul-entity to experience creation in all its diversity, so that each may return as a companion with the Creator.

The record of this experience becomes that part of an individual known as the akasha or soul record. It was these akashic records that the subconscious mind of Edgar Cayce was able to scan and comment upon through the life readings.

The record of planetary influences found in the akasha was explained as being emblematic of how an individual had reacted to various mental and emotional situations in the past. This was shown to be a present and continually evolving relationship:

> As to whether a soul is developed or retarded during a particular life depends on what the person holds as its ideal, and what it does in its mental and material relationships about that ideal.
>
> Life is a purposeful experience, and the place in which a person finds himself is one in which he may use his present abilities, faults, failures, virtues in fulfilling the purpose for which the soul decided to manifest in the three-dimensional plane.
>
> Know in thyself that there are immutable laws, and the universe about thyself is directed by laws set in motion from the beginning.
>
> So, as ye condemn, so are ye condemned. As ye forgive, so may ye be forgiven. As ye do unto the least of thy brethren, so ye do it unto thy Maker. These are laws; these are truths; they are unfailing. And because He may often appear slow in meting out results does not alter or change the law. An error, a fault, a failure, must be met. Though the heavens, the earth, may pass away, His word will not pass away. His word is the way, the truth, the light.

Each soul must pay to the last jot or tittle. (From the "Philosophy" chapter in *There Is a River.*)

Another intriguing aspect of Cayce's commentaries on planetary influences is found in response to a question on the validity of individuals' astrological charts.

For in about twenty percent of the populace at the present time [1939], it is dependent upon what the individuals have done with their urges *through* material sojourns.

As indicated through this channel, some are in keeping with the astrological charts, others are found to be partially so, others are diametrically opposed to same—because of the activities of the individuals. 5753-3

In short, Cayce at times both agreed or disagreed in part with traditional astrology. However, within the realm of his planetary discourses on soul development he presented implications that astrological matters are far more important than our scientifically oriented twentieth-century minds have allowed us to consider.

Before going to the readings' further explanation of akashic records and soul development, it would be well to note typical examples of entire readings with their planetary references. These have been included for study in appendix I. For those unfamiliar with astrological terms an additional appendix (II) and glossary are provided.

These examples give rise to numerous questions and possibilities for further study of subconscious psychic soul forces. It is toward that "great study," as the readings phrased it (3744-5), that this introduction is dedicated.

Jeffrey Furst, Editor
1967

1

The Language of the Readings

Both astrology and the Edgar Cayce readings have terminology and word usage that may not be familiar to all readers. This chapter will examine and clarify some basic concepts found in the readings that are important for understanding astrology. Additional astrological terms, including a brief overview of the planets, can be found in the glossary.

Personality and Individuality

The dictionary makes a very slight distinction between the meanings of these two words, saying that *per-*

sonality is individuality, and that an *individual* is one who "exists as a single, separate thing or being; separate and particular."

In the readings we are introduced to the novel idea that personality is one thing and individuality is another; further, that they may harmonize or be quite at variance with each other. Here the difference between these two is clearly stated:

> As to the appearances in the earth, not all may be given, but as a pattern may be indicated in the personality and individuality of this individual entity. Personality is that ye wish others to think and see. Individuality is that your soul prays, your soul hopes for, desires. They need not necessarily be one, but their purpose must be one, even as the Father, the Son and the Holy Spirit are one. So must body, mind and soul be one in purpose and in aim ... 5246-1

We are reminded here of the conflicts so often uncovered by psychiatrists, and by implication we suppose that everybody has these conflicts. Yet we also know of many people whom we call "well-balanced," and this must surely mean that their personalities and individualities are in harmony. Are they born with this harmony or do they achieve it? The readings indicate both. Balance comes from constant effort, through application of an ideal in every department of action and thought, including, probably, sojourns in planetary dimensions.

Students of orthodox astrology may parallel the meaning of the ascending sign and its degree with the Sun's position to understand personality and individuality better. The ascendant is thought of as pertaining to outside appearance and traits; the Sun in its sign is the inmost self, the spark of the Creator which, individual-

ized, has a purpose for coming to earth in that particular
sign. Ideally, one would reflect and support the other, in
a harmonious unity or balance.

Thus, as is indicated, may the individuality that
is the entity be brought in its activities so that its
personality may contribute to the factors necessary
to keep this entity in the direction needed. 5398-1

The individuality is the sum total of what the entity has done about those things that are creative or
ideal in its varied experiences in the earth. 4082-1

What happens when the personality and individuality are not in harmony, or in the process of being harmonized? For one thing, that entity is not influenced by his
or her planetary sojourns.

Urges termed astrological would be very far from
correct in this particular entity. For . . . the personality and the individuality of the entity are quite at
variance . . . seldom those that the entity takes into
its closest confidence. These bring for . . . a loneliness . . . and with even those the entity holds most
dear. 5246-1

Few people . . . really enjoy the companionship
of themselves. Not merely because they love themselves the less . . . But their thoughts . . . and the
emotions of the body are seldom in accord one with
the other—or their individuality and their personality don't reflect the same shadow in the mirror of
life. 3351-1

This discussion of personality and individuality is very
pertinent to the study of the total plan of soul evolution,

as described in the readings. According to this concept, between earth lives the soul-entity dwells, or sojourns, in planetary dimensions as a state of consciousness. From these sojourns come the mental urges that are carried over into earth lives, becoming a part of the individuality of the entity which is then expressed in the material world. The previous earth experiences create emotional urges, becoming the entity's personality in the earth lives.

The shadow of those things from the sojourns of this entity in Mercury, Jupiter, Saturn, Uranus, Venus and the influences . . . in the Sun and Moon, have their portion [influence] in the very relationships and activity of the entity. These [astrological influences] are but the mental urges that arise, and become as the individuality of an entity in expression in the material world . . . [On the other hand] the appearances in the earth through the various sojourns that are become active in the experience . . . at any one given place or position or appearance or period, are as but the personality in the entity's experience—and are as the urges from the emotions that have been created. 633-2

Latent and Manifested

The readings often started out by saying:

Yes, we have the entity and those relations with the universe and universal forces, as are latent in the present experience. 759-1

Or:

While these are rather given as a composite picture of latent and manifested characteristics, they

should be taken into consideration by those around
the entity. 305-3

Latent means "to lie hidden or concealed, undeveloped within a person or thing, as a quality or power; as
yet concealed or unrevealed." Manifested, then, means
the opposite of latent; it suggests a trait or trend—good,
bad, or indifferent—currently developing and being revealed.

It's clear that all the latent qualities, talents, etc., are
also innate, but the words are not synonymous. Probably all adults have innate qualities which are latent and
nonmanifested, as well as innate and manifested, and in
the making of these possibilities, the planets or planetary sojourns have had a definite and cooperative influence. We ourselves have made these potentials,
weaving them in and out, creatively or destructively,
from earthly emotional urges and from the planetary
mental urges carried over from realms of consciousness
outside the Earth.

We find that there are those urges latent and
manifested in the personalities and the individuality of this entity.

Personalities in the material plane arise from the
application of the entity's urges [emotional] in
earthly sojourns. Individualities arise from what an
entity would or does about the entity's ideal in a . . .
sojourn in the earth. 3211-2

Aspects

This is a familiar word to students of astrology. Textbooks list major and minor aspects, the major ones being the conjunction, the opposition, the square, the
trine, and the sextile.

Webster defines aspects in astrology to mean "the position of stars in relation to each other, or to the observer."

In this matter of aspects, the readings diverge rather drastically from textbook astrology. Aspects between planets in the natal chart or in the sunrise chart are seldom mentioned or given significance. From a study of hundreds of life readings, we found only one or two in which major aspects were mentioned. Aspects in connection with cycles in a person's life were referred to at times, with the explanation that such aspects involved the primary or secondary planets and thus stirred them to action.

Let us cite some extracts showing instances in which aspects between natal planets do not seem to be important.

As to astrological aspects, we find Jupiter as combined with Venus, Saturn and Uranus being the greater influences. 1931-1

In this chart, there are no major aspects between these planets. Jupiter is at 8 Leo, Venus at 20 Virgo (44 degrees between): Saturn at 2 Virgo, and Uranus at 29 Aquarius. The term Jupiter "as combined with Venus, Saturn and Uranus" seems to have a special meaning, but not in reference to a conjunction.

In the astrological aspects we find the entity headstrong from Mercury, yet very demure in its headstrongness, and oft sets itself to have its way— eventually has it and finds it isn't what was wanted at all. These [conditions] arise from those conflicting influences from Mercury, with Saturn.

Hence many changes in the aspects . . . 1406-1

From the use of the word *conflicting*, and Mercury with Saturn, we would expect a square or an opposition between Mercury and Saturn. This is not the case. Mercury is at 4 Aquarius and Saturn at 20 Libra; which is not close enough to be considered in trine, or 120 degrees, as astrology is taught. These two are 104 degrees apart, and orthodox astrology would not interpret these as interfering one with the other.

Other examples could be cited, but let us consider a reading which may explain what aspects really mean as far as present influences are concerned:

> Thus we find that the sojourns about the earth, during the interims between earthly sojourns, are called the astrological aspects. Not that an entity may have manifested physically on such planets, but [have manifested] in that consciousness which is the consciousness of that environ. And these [consciousnesses] have been accredited with certain potential influences in the mental aspect of an entity. 2144-1

> That absent from the material body is manifested in what we call astrological aspects, that become a phase of each and every soul—and are as signposts along the individual way.
>
> For . . . all of these are a part of thy heritage, thy innate urge; that arises from, and produces influences in, the material experiences in the present. 1745-1

> As to urges arising from astrological aspects, or the sojourns and activities when absent from materiality—we find these coming from the Moon, Mercury and Uranus. 2459-1

Traditional aspects between planets in the birth chart give little or no clue to which important planets will exert the most influence as indicated by the readings. A study of the most important planets mentioned in 150 children's readings shows that it is more than likely that there will be no orthodox astrological aspects between any of them.

Yet there seems to be considerable truth in the traditional belief in favorable and unfavorable aspects between planets. This is supported by the readings' own occasional mention and agreement with favorable trines or unfavorable squares when certain planets make these aspects by transit to natal planets. (See examples in the appendix.)

At the same time, a soul which has stayed out of earthly incarnations for hundreds of years still apparently has many opportunities to encounter favorable and unfavorable aspects to its dwelling place in the planetary dimensions. According to the way it has learned to handle these interplanetary vibrations, it comes to earth with various aspects—trines or squares, conjunctions, oppositions, or sextiles. Then, when in the earth the transiting planets attune to this pattern, the opportunity is given that entity to translate into three-dimensional action and reaction, good or bad, to consolidate or to shatter the pattern, to progress in soul growth, or to go backward.

2

Akasha: The Soul's Record of Evolutionary Progress

The Cayce life readings are unique in that a great part of the entire soul record, apparently, was scanned and commented upon during the reading. However, only a few planetary sojourns and previous earth lives were given for an individual, with selections made on the basis of what was influencing this particular life to the greatest extent.

How Cayce arrived at that point of being conscious of another individual's soul record was explained in a dream experience which he had twelve to fifteen times while giving readings. Here is one such description, as given by Cayce in the background material for 294-19:

I see myself as a tiny dot out of my physical body, which lies inert before me. I find myself oppressed by darkness, and there is a feeling of terrific loneliness. Suddenly, I am conscious of a white beam of light. As this tiny dot, I move upward following the light, knowing that I must follow it or be lost.

As I move along this path of light, I gradually become conscious of various levels upon which there is movement. Upon the first levels there are vague, horrible shapes, grotesque forms such as one sees in nightmares. Passing on, there begin to appear on either side misshapen forms of human beings with some part of the body magnified. Again there is a change and I become conscious of gray-hooded forms moving downward. Gradually, these become lighter in color. Then the direction changes and these forms move upward—and the color of the robes grows rapidly lighter. Next, there begin to appear on each side vague outlines of houses, walls, trees, etc., but everything is motionless. As I pass on, there is more light and movement in what appear to be normal cities and towns. With the growth of movement I become conscious of sounds, at first indistinct rumblings, then music, laughter, and singing of birds. There is more and more light, the colors become very beautiful, and there is the sound of wonderful music. The houses are left behind, ahead there is only a blending of sound and color. Quite suddenly, I come upon a hall of records. It is a hall without walls, without ceiling, but I am conscious of seeing an old man who hands me a large book—a record of the individual for whom I seek information.

Much is written about akashic records in metaphysical literature, and the emphasis is usually placed upon that part having to do with earth life. The Cayce readings make it quite clear that each soul is constantly adding to his or her record, whether "in the earth" or in planetary dimensions.

A typical reading, 1990-3, starts:

> Yes, we have the entity here, and those records that are a part of the entity's experience through the earth's plane, as well as through those interims of sojourn in the environs about the earth . . .

The akasha is not necessarily a total record of the individual's deeds mixed in with the whole of humanity, although a nation, as an entity, might have its own record. In fact, the Cayce readings indicate that this is true. The individual's soul record is one's own and like no other's.

> Each soul, each body, each individual, is an individual entity, and that done, that thought, becomes as a living record of the experience of that individual entity . . . in whatever sphere of consciousness this activity may be and is recorded upon the skein of time and space. 1292-1

> In giving, then, the astrological influences, these would vary considerably from that as would be seen from the spiritual—or the . . . soul experience in the earth's plane. Were this entity's experiences given from the purely astrological science, as accepted in many quarters, they would vary entirely from this [record] which may be given here, or that is viewed from here—for these are the Akashian records of the entity's or soul's development. As to how the present experience, with its environs, will be acted or influenced . . . will have little influence from the astrological standpoint. The entity will be governed

rather by the reaction of the experience in the earth's plane through its appearances, rather than astrological influences. 566-1

Here we see that all individuals are not affected equally by the planets. Some are more influenced than others; some few are not influenced at all. This latter situation is unusual, and we will come back to it.

The Will Is the Weaver

If there are two outlines in the record for each individual soul, how exactly do the two sets of influences function in the soul now incarnated in the earth? Of what do the influences consist? The following extracts explain:

Thus in giving the interpretations of the records here, we would give not only the environmental but also the hereditary influences: not merely from the material lineage but from the mental and spiritual. For these, too, are a part of the heritage of each and every soul.

While there are those influences [from the planets], those urges latent and manifested, know that no urge surpasses the will of the entity—the birthright given each soul that it may know itself to be itself and by choice become one with the Creator . . .

For, each soul . . . *is* a co-creator with the universal consciousness; making those activities for self, for others.

For, the astrological sojourns represent the mental or dream forces; while the material earthly sojourns represent the expression through the emotions—or the reaction . . . in expression, in experiences that may be had, may be sought, may be shunned . . . 2571-1

Or, stated in a different manner:

> It should be understood that the earthly-sojourn urges are [pertained] to the emotions; while the mental or innate urges are from the experiences of the soul in the environs about the earth.
>
> But these are merely urges or inclinations, not impelling forces, and these used in their proper relationships as warnings, or as those things to embrace, may be applied in the experience for helpful forces and influences.
>
> Know, however, that . . . what the will does about that which is set as its ideal in a mental, in a material or in the . . . spiritual [experiences]—and then having the courage to carry out that ideal—makes the difference between the constructive and creative . . . relationships and those that make one become rather as a drifter or a ne'er-do-well, or one very unstable and unhappy. 1401-1

To summarize: It seems that the emotions and the senses of the physical body are inherited by the entity from itself, from certain previous lives selected by the soul to manifest in this life. These emotions and sensory reactions make up our "personalities" (as differing from individualities) to be used in this life. Mental awarenesses, intuitions, and judgment of right and wrong come to be a part of the body because of the soul's life in spheres of consciousness outside the Earth or in planetary dimensions. Suspended over both, independent of both, is the will, which is free to use all factors at its command, either constructively or destructively. It has been suggested that the signs of the zodiac are patterns; the planets are the looms; the will is the weaver.

The entity's task in this life is to use will to harmonize the two patterns, earth and planetary urges, into a well-rounded whole. This does not mean scorning the material life and rejecting the emotional urges. It means making use of them, spiritualizing them, and making choices of conduct according to the entity's own ideal of what is constructive for oneself and others.

Apparently free will is carried over into planetary sojourns after passing from this life. But no matter how high the development is carried in these realms of other consciousnesses, the plan of soul evolution seems to call for the entity coming into earth life and manifesting the development according to this concept. The Earth and our planetary solar system was specifically designed to be a practice place for our thorough learning of free will's power. Reading 1719-1 states that astrological influences bring will into the experience in Earth—probably by natal planetary relationships (the birth chart) and by transits. It calls will "that factor which may be trained, even as the mental forces," and "that developer in the material force" on the Earth, or as a balance-wheel between the Earth urges and the innate soul urges.

Free Will in Other Dimensions

Many philosophers have doubted that the soul has free will in other dimensions, yet the readings have stated that will is manifested and applied in constructive ways outside the earth.

> For Life is a continuous experience. And the mind, the soul, the will, are those influences that act through the material manifestation, for the improvement, the development, or for the retardment to the whole of the experience.
>
> For each soul enters each experience for a development, that it may be prepared to dwell with that it seeks as its goal.

Hence the necessity of each entity . . . setting its ideal in each experience.

Hence we find in the developments through those activities of an entity in a material sojourn or through an astrological experience are but the evolution, or making practical. For it is not what an individual or an entity may proclaim that counts, but what each soul . . . does about that it has set as its ideal in relationships to . . . [other] individuals about same. 1235-1

Yet may this entity be set apart. For through its experiences in the earth, it has advanced from a law degree to that which may not even necessitate a reincarnation in the earth. Not that it has reached perfection but there are realms for instruction if the entity will hold to that ideal . . . Remember, there are material urges [here] and there are materials in other consciousnesses not three-dimensional alone. 5366-1

Thus we find this entity—as each entity— is in the present the result of that the entity has applied of Creative influences . . . in every phase of its experience. Thus it makes for that called by some karma, by others racial hereditary forces . . . [which] (as are accepted) are in their reality the activities of the *mind* of the entity in its choices through the experiences in the material, in the mental, in the spiritual planes. 1796-1

Emotions and the Glandular Centers

Emotions, our inheritance from sojourns in the Earth, are complicated by their tie-in with the glandular structure. The following excerpt suggests that a distinction be made:

The awarenesses are a pattern of that we call astrological aspects. Not because the entity in— physical consciousness sojourned in any of the planets that are a part of this present solar experience, but each planet is accredited with certain environmental influences that are represented in the characteristics of each individual soul.

Thus, as we find in this entity: they [the planets] give expression in the abilities which find manifestation in the material body through developments or attunements in the glandular system of the body *for* material expression.

Thus upon the skein of time and space is the record of each soul made. In patience, in persistence may such be read . . .

As to the appearances or sojourns in the earth— these we find expressed or manifested in the material body through the senses. Do understand, do interpret the difference between the emotions that arise from the sensory system and those that arise from the *glandular* system alone. True, physically these interchange, yet one [the glandular] represents the *whole* of the development, the other [sensory] represents the step-by-step activity by an entity in its activity through the material world. 2620-2

The akashic record is embodied in the glandular system for the purpose of the entity's material expression "In patience, in persistence." The practice of meditation arouses the seven glandular centers if and when the purpose is to draw nearer to the divine source. The centers are the connection among the physical, the mental, and the spiritual.

The spiritual contact is through the glandular
forces of creative energies . . . Thus we find the connection, the association of the spiritual being with
the mental self, at those centers [glandular] from
which the reflexes react to all of the organs, all of
the emotions, all of the activities of a physical body.
263-13

For a more detailed study of meditation, the endocrine glands, and their physical-spiritual connections,
see the booklet *Meditation—Gateway to Light* by Elsie
Sechrist. Each of the seven glands, or psychic centers, is
said to be attuned or related to a planet, as follows:

The pituitary (Jupiter)
The pineal (Mercury)
The thyroid (Uranus)
The thymus (Venus)
The adrenals (Mars)
The lyden gland (Neptune)
The gonads or sex glands (Saturn)

These relationships and many others were brought
out in a series of readings (281) explaining the symbol-
ogy of the Book of Revelation of St. John the Divine.

3

The Great Plan of Soul Evolution

The word *cosmogony* is used to describe theories of the physical origin or generation of the universe, and many respectable scientists indulge in such conjecture. Their theories vary, but guesses concerning the unknown are considered academically acceptable when scientists are guessing.

Cosmology, on the other hand, means the philosophy of the nature and first principles of the universe. Physical scientists generally decline to comment on these unknowns, leaving such speculation to philosophers and calling it *metaphysics*. But why was the universe made? What is the meaning behind the creation of so many

suns and solar systems, stars, galaxies, nebulae? What is
the purpose of our own solar system? Are there others
with the same purpose? What is the relationship of our
own solar system to others? And most important to us:
What is our relationship to these various systems? Or
why, essentially, do we exist?

These are questions that preoccupy the philosopher
and theologian alike, and the answers are suggested in
the life readings given by Edgar Cayce. In these records
humanity's relationship to its solar system is shown as a
plan for soul evolution that is vast and inspiring in scope.
According to this information, humans are very personally related to their limited universe, our solar system.
We are caught up in its purpose, and it is involved in our
purpose for being here. There is interaction between individuals on Earth and the planets, Sun, and Moon. We
influence them, they influence us. This influence is
somewhat different from what is taught by traditional
astrology.

For us to know something of this plan is to understand
ourselves and others better. Here, the principles of the
Christian ethic become intensified and very personal in
meaning. Thus, all people can be seen truly as brothers
and sisters involved in the struggle for soul evolution and
growth. Our solar system was created for humankind's evolution.

As has been indicated by some, ye are part and
parcel of a universal consciousness or God—and
thus all that is within the universal consciousness,
or the universal awareness; as the stars, the planets,
the sun, the moon. Do ye rule them or they rule
thee? They were made for thy own use, as an individual—yea, that is the part [they play], the thought
thy Maker, thy Father-God thinks of thee.

For ye are as a corpuscle in the body of God; thus a co-creator with Him, in what ye think, in what ye do. 2794-3

The next reading becomes more specific about the influence of our solar system:

When the heavens and the earth came into being, this meant the universe as the inhabitants of the earth know same; yet there are many suns in the universe—those even about which our sun, our earth, revolve; and all are moving toward some place—yet space and time appear to be incomplete.

Then time and space are but one. Yet the sun, that is the center of this particular solar system, is the center; and, as has been . . . known of old, it [the sun] is that about which the earth and its companion planets circulate or evolve [revolve].

The beginnings of the understanding of these [facts], and their influence upon the lives of individuals, were either thought out, evolved or interpreted by those of old, without the means of observing same as considered today necessary in order to understand.

Astronomy is considered a science, and astrology as foolishness. Who is correct? One [astrology] holds that because of the position of the earth, the sun, the planets, they are balanced one with another in some manner, some form, yet that they have nothing to do with man's life or the expanse of life, or the emotions of the physical being in the earth.

Then why and how do the effects of the sun *so* influence other life in the earth and not affect *man's* life, man's emotions?

As the sun has been set as the ruler of this solar

system, does it not appear to be reasonable that it *has* an effect upon the inhabitants of the earth, as well as upon plant and mineral life in the earth . . .

Thus we find given [in the Bible], the sun and the moon and the stars were made also—this being the attempt of the writer to convey to the individual the realization that there *is* an influence in their activity! For, remember, they—the sun, the moon, the planets—have their marching orders from the Divine, and they move in same.

Man alone is given that birthright of free will. He alone may defy his God. 5757-1

Thus we come to the idea of the human being as a possible and actual rebel, with the need for this awareness as part of one's soul evolution; hence, the need for the solar system, for Earth lives, and planetary sojourns. Our defiance and rebellion came about when "souls projected themselves into matter [Earth] and thus brought that conscious awareness of themselves entertaining the ability of creating without those forces of the spirit of truth." (5755-2) They became more and more material-minded, or selfish, and lost the feeling of oneness with the Father; the pattern was flawed—the purpose for which they had been created—to be companions with the Father. Souls had to start the long way back to Him, learning to use their minds and wills in creative instead of selfish ways, with love instead of hate, with patience and faith instead of hasty judging. These virtues were to be applied to self, in guiding one's thoughts and actions inward, as well as toward other souls.

The Earth became a "practice place" where souls were to demonstrate what they had learned in other lives, combined with lessons from other dimensions of consciousness represented by the planets when absent from the earth in these other dimensions. Each planet represented a portion of these lessons to be learned—each a cluster of spheres or planes or vibratory dimensions of consciousness in which the soul was to dwell and become aware.

> Hence we find how, as ye draw your patterns from these [the sun and planets], that they become a part of the whole [individual or solar-whole]. For ye are *relatively* related to all that ye have contacted in materiality [the earth], mentality, spirituality! All of these are a portion of thyself in the material plane.
>
> In taking form [material] they become a mental body with its longings for its home, with right and righteousness [heaven].
>
> Then that ye know as thy mental self is the form taken, with all of its variations as combined from the things it has been [has experienced] within, without, and in relationship to the activities in materiality as well as in the spheres or various consciousnesses . . . 5755-1

We Affect the Solar System

Listeners to reading 5757-1 felt many questions in their minds and hearts about humanity's disobedience really affecting the solar system. In answers to their questions, the reading proceeded to amplify many points. The sun, it stated, was made for the purpose of shedding light and heat upon God's children in the Earth and is of the same composition of which we are made: solid, liquid, and vapor, or the various stages of human consciousness or activity. Describing the Sun's stability, the reading states that it was:

> . . . commanded to march, to show forth the

Lord's glory, His beauty, His mercy, His hope—yea,
His patience . . .

Questions were asked about sunspots, and the reading stated:

> . . . reflected upon even the face of the sun those
> turmoils and strifes that have been and that are the
> sin of man . . .
> How do they [sunspots] affect man? How does a
> cross word affect thee? How [do] anger, jealousy,
> hate, animosity, affect thee *as* a son of God? . . . If
> thou art the recipient of same from others, thy
> brethren, how does it affect thee? Much as that confusion which is caused upon the earth by that which
> appears as a sunspot the disruption of communications of all natures . . .
> Then, what are the sunspots? A natural consequence of that turmoil which the sons of God in the
> earth reflect upon same [the sun].
> Thus they oft bring confusion to those who become aware of same . . .
> *Know* [then] that thy mind—thy *mind*—is the
> builder! As what does thy soul appear? A spot, a blot
> upon the sun? or as that which giveth light unto
> those who sit in darkness, to those who cry aloud
> for hope? 5757-1

Changes in the universe and in the relative positions
of planets, stars, and zodiac are attributed to human activity, good and bad.

> As in the studies of the entity it is seen that the
> soul of man is a mere speck in space, yet the soul
> . . . is that vital force or activity which is everlasting.
> Though the earth, though the stars, may pass away;

though there may be changes in the universe as to the relative position, these are brought about by those combinations of that speck of human activity as relative *to* the soul's expression in any sphere of experience. 1297-1

How Can Astrology Help?

In reading 3744-4, this question was asked: "Is it proper for us to study the effects of the planets on our lives in order to better understand our tendencies and inclinations, as influenced by the planets?" The answer was a resounding yes.

> When studied aright, [it is] very, very, very much so. How aright then? In that influence as is seen in the influence of the knowledge already obtained by mortal man. Give more of that into the lives, giving the understanding *that the will must be the ever guiding factor to lead man on, ever upward.* 3744-4

The part that will plays in our evolution along the Christ path toward companionship with God cannot be overemphasized. The Earth is a battleground on which mental and spiritual urges from planetary sojourns meet and vanquish, or harmonize with, the emotional urges from past lives.

The umpire or arbiter in this battle, the general who marshals both sides and directs the outcome, is the will of the soul-entity. Free will is the constant, the God-spark. This fact is reiterated, from many points of view and in various languages, in the following extracts:

> . . . *will*, that factor which may be trained, even as the mental forces, and *will*, that developer in the material force, being the balance between influ-

ences . . . innately built or those of that karmic influence that makes for the *freedom* of the mental
being; for in Truth one finds freedom, for he that
findeth the Truth is free indeed. 1719-1

Astrological aspects may or may not become a
part of the experience physically for the entity. For
these are merely urges, and the will—that which
designates God's creation of man from the rest of
the animal world—rules as to what an individual
soul does with opportunities in relationships with
the fellow man. 3340-1

For will is that factor . . . which gives the ability to
choose that as may be for the development or the
retardment. For, as has so oft been indicated, there
is today—now—set before each and every entity,
every soul, that which is life and death, good and
evil. Each entity, each soul, chooses in its manifestations. 1646-2

Not that there are not definite helps to be at-
tained from astrology; but those who live by same
the more oft are controlled rather than controlling . . .
Astrology is a fact, in most instances. But astrological aspects are but signs, symbols. *No influence*
is of greater value or of greater help than the *will* of
an individual.
Use such directions [from the planets] as stepping-stones. Do not let them become stumbling
stones in thy experience. 815-6

It seems reasonable to believe that realms of consciousness through which souls have developed will be
reflected, at least partially, in the planetary patterns of

their horoscopes. If this is so, we can get clues to our mental and spiritual selves by studying this record of choices.

Planets Were Made for Humanity

Rather, then, than the stars *ruling* the life, the life should rule the stars—for man was created a little bit higher than all the rest of the whole universe, and is capable of harnessing, directing, enforcing, the laws of the universe. 5-2

This plan for our soul evolution is also stated in the following excerpt:

The earth is the Lord's and the fullness thereof. The universe He called into being for purposes that the individual soul, that might be one with Him, would have . . . those influences for bringing this to pass or to be in the experience of every soul.

For hath it not been given that the Lord thy God hath not willed that any soul should perish? but He hath prepared with every temptation a means, a way of escape.

Hence . . . the period of the entrance [birth] is not ruled by the position [of sun and planets] but it may be judged by the position as to the influence . . . upon an entity's experience because of the entity's application of self's abilities relative to its position in the universal scheme of things . . . 1347-1

This means that some of the progress, at least, can be judged in reference to the horoscope, with its rising sign and angles, and by a certain number (not all) of the planets. This progress can be judged by the manner in which a soul has applied its abilities previously, according to "the universal scheme of things," or constructively.

Variations Between Horoscope Readings and Life Readings

There is a difference, however, between information derived from a horoscope reading and that from a life reading.

(Q) What is a horoscope reading?

(A) That in which the planets and their relative forces [here] to do with the planets that control the actions without respect of will or without respect of the earthly existences through which the body has passed.

(Q) Do horoscope readings include former appearances in the earth plane?

(A) Not at all. The former appearances and the relation of the solar forces in the Universe have their relations to what might be termed life readings, [while an astrology chart indicates] the science of the solar system and the relation to various phases of earth's existence [as it] may mean for anyone. In life existence in earth's plane, and the entity's relation to other sphere [as in a life reading] a different condition, for the sojourn in other spheres than earth's plane controls more the conditions or the *urge* of the individual, just as we see . . . an individual controlled by the surroundings, or by the circumstances . . . yet the urge, the latent forces [of] two individuals raised under the same environment, of the same blood, would have different urges. These received from experiences the spirit entity gains in other spheres, correlated with that of its present circumstance . . . for . . . a horoscope is only the mathematical calculation of earth's position in the Universe at any given time, while in the life reading would be the correlation of the individual with a given time and place, with its relative force as applied and received through other spheres and manifested in earth's sphere in the flesh, and the development being the extenuation of the soul's development manifested in the earth plane . . . 254-21

Necessity for Planetary Experiences

Before considering the actual urges from the planets working through the individual in daily life, let us consider the question of why there are eight planets, Sun, and Moon. We are told in many of the readings that the soul-entity outside the earth plane may even pass on to other solar systems, through Arcturus, Polaris, or Septimus, or may choose to return to Earth.

> . . . though there may be worlds, many universes, even much as to solar systems, greater than our own that we enjoy in the present, this earthly experience on this earth is a mere speck when considered even with our own solar system. Yet the soul of man, thy soul, encompasses *all* in this solar system, or in others . . .
>
> But hast thou conceived—or canst thou conceive—the requirements of the influence to meet all the idiosyncrasies of a *single* soul? How many systems would it require? In thyself we find oft one friend for this, another for that, another for this relationship, another for the prop, another to arouse. Yet all are the work of His hand, are thine to possess, thine to use . . .
>
> Is God's hand short, that there would not be all that each soul would require? 5755-2

Planetary Dimensions

Various attempts have been made to describe the soul's spiritual dwellings outside the earth plane or in the interims between death and birth. Some feel that the soul goes directly to some other planet and manifests there in the same way in which it manifested on the earth plane; that it inhabits each planet, as the material body inhabits the earth.

This is a misconception, according to the readings, and yet it cannot be definitely stated what is meant by planes or spheres or dimensions of consciousness or vibratory centers. The Earth is a three-dimensional planet, and while we are here, we think mostly in three-dimensional terms. In some dream states, the soul may be in a four-dimensional state. The readings state that there are eight dimensions.

When we speak of the Earth being a three-dimensional environment, we mention length, breadth, and height. Yet the readings define the three dimensions as time, space, and patience.

> For the entity finds itself a body, a mind, a soul—three; or the earth consciousness as a three-dimensional plane in one.
> So man's concept of the Godhead is three-dimensional—Father, Son and Holy Spirit. The communication or the activity or the motivating force we find is three-dimensional—time, space and patience. Neither of these exists in fact, except in the concept of the individual as it may apply to time or space or patience. 4035-1

Vibrations Explained

We now have a number of terms describing planetary

dimensions: spheres, planes, phases of consciousness, stages of the condition, dimensions of consciousness, etc. To these we add the term *vibrations*, which is perhaps the most understandable description of all. In the following reading planetary vibrations are explained by drawing a parallel with the vibrations one collects, absorbs, and builds by dwelling and working in a special environment, such as a college.

> Just as the entity's attending this or that university . . . would make for a parlance peculiar unto itself. Even though individuals may study the same line of thought, one attending Harvard, another Yale, another Oxford, another Stanford, another the University of Arizona, they each would carry with them the vibrations created by their very activity in those environs.
>
> In the same way, emotions arise from . . . activity in a particular sojourn, and are called the *spirit* of the institution to which the entity may have carried itself . . . So we find those astrological sojourns making these vibrations or impressions in the present entity. 633-2

We are affected by planetary vibrations (transits of planets) during our lifetimes because we have attuned ourselves to them during sojourns in those environs. The portion of our personality vibrations represented by a planet's vibrations which we have acquired reacts to the movements of a transiting planet.

This concept of the effect of planets seems to be what is referred to here:

> Then there are the sojourns in other realms of the solar system which represent certain attributes. Not that ye maintain a physical earth-body in Mercury,

Venus, Jupiter, Uranus or Saturn, but there is an
awareness or a consciousness in those realms when
absent from the body, and the response to the position those planets occupy in this solar system . . .
    Thus ye oft find in thy experiences that places,
peoples, things and conditions are a part of self as if
ye were in the consciousness of same. 2823-1

But what has all this to do with the plan of soul evolution?

    Each entity is a part of the universal whole. All
knowledge, all understanding that has been a part
of the entity's consciousness, then, is a part of the
entity's experience.
    Thus the unfoldment in the present is merely be-
coming aware of that experience through which the
entity, either in body or in mind, has passed in a
consciousness. 2823-1

4

The Planets

For when thou beholdest the glory of the Father in the earth, how ORDERLY are all His glories! Hast thou watched the Sun in his orbit? How ORDERLY are those places of *the inhabitation of the souls of men,* even in thine OWN— in thine OWN—understanding of this solar system! How ORDERLY is there brought into manifestation day and night, heat and cold, spring and summer . . . canst thou, as His son, be more unorderly than He and expect His blessings? [Author's italics] 440-14

The readings refer to the planets as vibratory centers or the "places of the inhabitation of the souls of men" between earth lives. Is there awareness in these vibratory centers? The readings indicate that there is.

Thus as the soul passes from the aspects about the material environs or the earth, we find the astrological aspects are represented as stages of consciousness; given names that represent planets or centers, or crystallized activity.

Not that flesh and blood, as known in the earth, dwell therein; but in a consciousness, with the form and manner as befits the environ. 1650-1

Also during the interims between such [material] sojourns, there are consciousnesses or awarenesses. For the soul is eternal and it lives on, it has a consciousness and awareness of that which it has been built. 2620-2

Reading 5755-1 refers to Uranus's "tone or attunement"; hence we must add vibration of sound and color to our total concept of planetary dwelling places. Many other readings allude to the vibrations of music and color in reference to the planets.

. . . though, of course, the tonal vibration is that which *produces* color . . . color and tone are just different rates of vibration. 2779-1

Reading 281-30 states that vibration is the essence or basis of color. Another reading, 5755-1, gives the summation:

For it is not strange that music, color and vibration are all a part of the planets, just as the planets are a part—and a pattern—of the whole universe.

Specific colors and notes of the scale have been attributed to specific planets but not enough research has been done to cite these here, or even to say that just one color belongs to a given planet. Light and dark red, for instance, are mentioned, as are hues, tinges, mixtures, etc. It could be that the planets' colors form a rainbow in which (to the human eye) one color merges into another. And if each planet represents a musical note of vibration, then there are sharps and flats, chords, melodies, counterpoint, and symphonies—the "music of the spheres" referred to in the readings.

Because we are equipped to see colors and to hear music, the concept of the planets as centers of vibration seems more satisfactory than the concept of "dimensions," which is also a term used in the readings.

Why are eight vibrations needed in the planetary scheme for soul development?

> For, without passing through each and every stage of development, there is not the correct vibration to become one with the Creator . . .
>
> Then, in the many stages of development, throughout the universal or in the great system of the universal forces, each stage of development [is] made manifest through flesh, which is the testing portion of the universal vibration. In this manner then, and for this reason, all [are] made manifest in flesh and [there is] development, through the eons of time, space, and [that] *called* eternity. 900-16

The individual who requested the following reading was evidently interested in numerology, as one question asked about having a soul number. The answer stated that only in the earth plane does an entity have a soul number. Another question was whether the entity has an opportunity to change its rate of vibration in planetary sojourns. This the answer:

> Each planetary influence vibrates at a different rate

of vibration. An entity entering that influence enters that vibration; [it is] not necessary that he change, but it is the grace of God that he may! It is part of the universal consciousness, the universal law. 281-55

There is a great deal of individual variation in each soul's awarenesses of the planets.

Hence the entity passes along those stages that some have seen as planes, some have seen as steps, some have seen as cycles, and some have experienced as places. 5755-1

Textbooks and the Readings

Astrological textbooks attribute definite and specific meanings as well as influences to the various planets. How do these meanings compare with the readings? There are striking similarities, but also notable differences. These will be pointed out as each planet is discussed. It should be remembered, though, that even the astrologers do not agree on every point.

MERCURY

Textbooks say that Mercury is the planet of mind, reason, and intellect; the planet of speech, writing, and communication; governs the arms, hands, lungs, tongue, intestines, sense of sight.

Notice that Mercury is associated directly with the other senses as well as sight: with the hands, therefore, the sense of touch; with the tongue, therefore, sense of taste and the associated sense of smell. The sense of hearing is also attributed to Mercury.

Ellen McCaffery, M.A., in her *Graphic Astrology* (Macoy Publishing Co., Richmond, Va., 1952) discusses Mercury thus:

Astrology shows us that the planet Mercury governs the mind. We reap our reward according to the way we use our mind. If Mercury comes to the planet Mars [occupies by transit the same degree as Mars in birthchart], we can use this energy [Mars] to fight people, or we can do some constructive work. If Mercury comes to Saturn, we can be melancholy and mean, or we can use the rays of Saturn to help us delve down into the structure of things. It all depends upon how we discipline our minds, just what we will do when the planets move. The more unevolved the soul, the more it responds to adverse planetary vibrations. (p. 16)

The readings repeatedly maintain that "mind is the builder," and this is in accordance with orthodox teachings in astrology. However, a divergence lies in the readings' wider and more comprehensive concepts of the mind of humankind.

Hence we find that the mental body is both finite and infinite, a part of self and yet a part of the universal consciousness—or the mind of the Maker. 1650-1

Mercury brings the high mental abilities; the faculties that at times may become the developing for the soul or at others turned to the aggrandizement of selfish interests.
For the entity is among those who have entered the earth during those years when there was the great entrance of those who have risen high in their abilities, and who are then passing through those periods when there must be application of the will, else the very abilities that have been maintained in the Sun and Mercurian influences will become as stumbling blocks . . . 633-2

Why is mind the builder? Because it exercises choice between good and evil, or the delicate balance between the most-good with the least-evil. Will motivates that choice, and mind controls will.

Mind is the factor that is in direct opposition of will. Mind being that control of, or being the spark of the Maker, the *will* [that which makes one an] individual when we reach the plane of man. 3744-2

Mercury, which symbolizes mental consciousness, is the catalyst by which all eight planetary vibrations are harmonized, harnessed, assimilated, and put to full constructive use on the earth plane, if advancement is to be made.

As a matter of fact, it is impossible to consider any one planet entirely apart from the others which influence the dominant one. Note the following explanation of Mercury's role:

In Jupiter's forces we find the great ennobling, those conditions that would bring the monies and forces of good into the life.

In Neptune, those of the mysticism, mystery, spiritual insight, spiritual development.

The Mercury influence of mental understanding of each.

Then, with a mental insight into the operative elements of ennobling, of virtues, the good, of beautiful, with the mysteries of the universal forces, given understanding, brings development to the soul's forces. For *the soul feeds upon that environment to which the mind guides and directs . . .* [Author's italics] 900-14

In the readings, Mercury is associated with the pineal gland.

VENUS

Venus is the Earth's closest neighbor, not counting the Moon. McCaffery says it "manifests all the things of the world glorified under the radiance of the Sun. It betokens the principle of love on earth; of attraction, joy, gifts, and benefits." It signifies, at its best, harmony, sweetness, gentleness, and the spirit of refinement and good taste. It encourages us to make our surroundings beautiful, and so governs the arts. In music it rules melody rather than harmony, which pertains more to the mental Mercury. It is the peacemaking planet. Books on astrology call Venus "the Lesser Benefic," the planet through which many fortunate and good things come to the individual.

The readings agree with all these concepts of the role of Venus's influence upon the soul-self because of its sojourns in those vibrations. The dominant planet—the one from which the soul took flight to come to Earth—will show forth its influence through other planets named as influential in the life reading, and fortunate indeed is the soul which arrived from Venus. Here are a few excerpts:

> One of a tender, loving disposition; that may be ruled or reasoned with through love, obedience or duty; yet may not be driven . . . through sheer force or fear of corporal punishment.
>
> In this influence also we will find that sympathy—or . . . being able under any circumstances to make for the alleviating of hardships, pains, or such conditions in the experience of others—will ever be *appealing* to the entity. 309-1

> In the astrological aspects, we find that, through influences from sojourns in the Venus environs, the entity is a lover of beauty, especially of song . . .

should be given training . . . [for] the awakening of
the entity in those influences . . . for the use of the
entity's voice in *praise* and in thanksgiving . . .

Hence all things that have to do with phases of
man's ability to express in beautiful ways and man-
ners will be of interest . . . whether pertaining to
nature, to voice or song, or even to art subjects.
1990-3

In the following reading, a significant statement is
made regarding beauty and the home, for a child who
entered the earth plane through forces of Venus.

As Venus is the ruling influence in the experience,
we find that the home will be, should be, the channel through which the greater abilities . . . may be
made manifest.

Not that there are not abilities in music and art
. . . But making an artistic home, making a home
that is the expression of beauty in *all* its phases, is
the greater career of *any* individual soul. This [the
home] is the closer expression of that which has
been manifested [by] man's advent into materiality.
2571-1

Here is an enlarged concept of the influences from
Venus's for which are primarily love; but love, too, has its
extremes.

In Venus the body-form is near to that [which is]
in the three-dimensional plane. For it is what may
be said to be rather *all*-inclusive! For it is what ye
would call love—which, to be sure, may be licen-
tious, selfish; which also may be so large, so inclu-
sive as to take on the less of self and more of the
ideal, more of that which is *giving*.

What is love? Then what is Venus? It is beauty, love, hope, charity—yet all of these have their extremes. But these extremes are not in the expressive nature or manner . . . found in that tone or attunement of Uranus [the planet of extremes]; for they (in Venus) are more in the order that they blend one with another. 5755-1

According to the readings, the gland associated with the planet Venus is the thymus. Some physiologists and pathologists say that this gland has atrophied in the adult body, or at least has shrunk considerably. Could this be a commentary on our lives?

MARS

The next planet beyond the Earth is Mars, whose orbit encloses the Sun-Mercury-Venus-Earth group.

Mars is said to be the planet of energy or sex. It rules creativeness, construction, invention, ceaseless activity, force, power, work, strife, war, and death. McCaffery says, "It declares the ceaseless, ever-new stream of energy which brings about new forms; hence it is said to rule the sex energies. When the rays of Mars play upon the Moon, they single out the instinct of pugnacity, anger, and self-assertiveness. Mars can make these into very destructive forces, or it can exalt them into the noblest virtues—courage, strength of character, self-confidence, and power."

Further interpretations of Mars's attributes given in the textbooks are: rulership over adventure, sports activities, and businesses; the sense of taste; its stone, the bloodstone; its color, red; its day of the week, Tuesday.

With the majority of these attributes the Cayce readings agree, except that the readings emphasize the *inwardness* or psychological urge of planetary vibrations rather than outward events. For some entities or souls, however, the vibrations of Mars are scarcely felt or easily subdued, because they have mastered the impulses to anger, selfishness, and aggression. Such souls may be said to have a "good Mars," as the astrologers would put it. This writer, in examination of dozens of accurate birth charts, has not been able to find that such a *good Mars* has only good aspects (trine, sextile, etc.). We would conclude that the good attributes of Mars in any present earth-plane existence result from the quick learning of the lessons for which the soul came to earth, lessons inherent in the Mars vibrations.

The following excerpts from the readings delineate the attributes cited above:

> Astrologically we find Mars, Mercury, Venus, and Jupiter—and note their importance. [Their order—entity entered from Mars.] Anger may upset the body and cause a great deal of disturbance, to others as well as self.
>
> Be angry, but sin not. You will learn it only in patience and self-possession. 3621-1

> Astrologically, we find quite a few variations in the entity's experiences. Besides Mercury, we find Neptune, Saturn, and Mars always stepping in. Hence it has appeared to the entity at times that many of the associates . . . can get mad easier than anybody. Yet the entity may be mad and sin not. Righteous anger is a virtue. He that has no temper is very weak, but he that controls not his temper is *much* worse. This ye experience . . . at times. This is active patience. Don't think it, much less do it. For as a man thinketh in his heart, so is he. 3416-1

> For the inclinations from the Martian influences are for anger to arise easily in the experiences when

the entity is fraught [frustrated] in its activities, in the associations, or its determinations. And it usually has its way, unless there is reason and love and care and precaution shown by those who direct the developing or formative periods. 1434-1

Lest we forget that the planetary urges—strong as they may be—cannot and should not rule the life, consider this reading for a three-year-old-child. Warnings are given to the parents at the very beginning that the child not be allowed to play with fireworks and firearms, "For, Mars is adverse to Jupiter in the experience . . . "

Astrological aspects may or may not become a part of the experience physically for the entity. For these are merely urges, and the will—that which designates God's creation of man from the rest of the animal world—rules, as to what an individual soul does with opportunities, in relationship with his fellow man.

In Mars we find this activity. The entity will never be called lazy. May be called stubborn at times, but this, too, may be directed—not by undue punishment but by reasoning with an appealing to the entity . . . Not that there should be a prize for goodness, but remember that virtue has its own reward, even for those attempting to direct and train children. 3340-1

In the readings, the gland associated with Mars is the adrenal.

JUPITER

The planet next farther out from Mars, or the third, counting Earth as number one, is Jupiter.

Jupiter is called "the Greater Benefic" in astrology textbooks, and to it are attributed good fortune, wealth, social position, happiness, etc. An astrology magazine names Jupiter as patron of expansion, gain, and optimism; controlling the liver, hips, thighs, sense of smell; its colors, green and purple; its metal, tin; and its gem, the turquoise. McCaffery comes closest to the readings' description of Jupiter when she says, "The emotions can become beautiful under Jupiter, but they are always expanded in scope. The Moon and Venus may express tenderness to one, but Jupiter may express benevolence, kindness, and generosity to everyone . . . Jupiter seeks the cause and basis of actions . . . Because the planet inquires into motives and purposes, it is essentially the planet of the judge and the lawmaker. Under its rays, the moral qualities within us begin to develop. Largeness of outlook is cultivated. There is nothing petty or small about Jupiter. It stands for soul growth, expansion, and magnanimity."

The last two sentences coincide with what the readings say about the *inner urge or attunement* of the soul which entered the earth plane, with Jupiter as one of the affecting planets and, moreover, affecting it favorably.

Speaking generally, however, the readings stress universality and ennoblement as Jupiter's vibrations, showing how these turn the soul-self toward large groups of people, even nations. The following excerpts show how Jupiter's expansive influence works through the other planets named as affecting one's life:

> In Venus with Jupiter, we see those abilities to appreciate those things and those experiences that are as from the realm of the universal consciousness, as indicated in the song of the bird, the music of the stream, the beauty of nature; yet, with Jupiter these become universal forces, or those activities in the material plane will have to do with groups and

masses, rather than with individuals; though it may be individual in its application. 2869-1

From the Jupiterian sojourn, we find not only the benevolent, but the adverse forces. For while Venus *with* the Jupiterian brings the enjoyment of the beautiful in ways that would pertain to a universal consciousness or activity, the adverse in Mars indicates that wrath . . . may bring those things to cause the influence to be in a reverse manner . . . 1990-3

As we find . . . those influences in the astrological aspects show Jupiter as the ruling force [entity entered from Jupiter].

Hence . . . the entity's activities must have to do with the many . . .

Those influences in Venus make for an open, frank, loving disposition; making for friends in most any walk or every walk of life. 1442-1

In the latter reading, Venus and Neptune were cited as secondary and tertiary influences, and Neptune's influences were also described as expansive, showing how Jupiter works through the other important planets.

In another instance the entity was said to have entered the earth plane from Jupiter, with Venus, Mercury, and Mars affecting the life. Notice how the urges from Venus, Mercury, and Mars are *broadened* in outlook through Jupiter's influence:

In Jupiter, we find the great ennobling influences, the broad-mindedness, the ability to consider others, the universal consciousnesses that are a part of the entity's unfoldment.

We find in Venus that unusual attraction that the opposite sex will have for the entity, and the entity for the opposite sex. Hence relationships in such should be the problems, as well as the studies and the guidance through the periods especially in the next cycle—or during the next seven years for the entity.

In Mercury and Mars, we find the energetic activities of mind and of body, and at times appearing oppressive in the experience of others as related to the entity as a meddler. Yet these are benevolent forces, if those activities . . . of the entity are used and analyzed in that way of aiding the entity in its preparation though such experiences . . . 2890-2

A "good Jupiter," say the textbooks, brings money and this world's goods, comfort, and perhaps luxury. The readings seem to agree with this.

In Jupiter we find the associations making for those tendencies for large groups . . . in relationships with the entity. This makes also for those inclinations that . . . will be great amounts of this world's goods [in the entity's experiences] . . . The training also then not only in its teen age [years] but throughout its development . . . as to the use of same [wealth], as being lent from Creative Forces and energies, and not for self-indulgence . . . 1206-3

The readings say that Jupiter rules the pituitary gland.

SATURN

The concept of Saturn, the fourth planet outward counting the Earth as one, is one thing in the textbooks and another in the Cayce readings. Here is one of the greatest discrepancies with traditional astrology. Let us carefully examine the differences.

One astrology magazine says: "Saturn has dominion

over age, caution, limitation, stabilization, the bones, spleen, teeth, sense of hearing, head, dark colors, Saturday."

McCaffery says, among other things, that Saturn is the recluse, the scientist, anything highly organized or condensed into capsule form, the principle of contraction and solidification. "Saturn governs organization and, therefore, is said to rule the governments of nations, and the executive bodies of large corporations . . . Saturn gives depth to the character and firmness of conviction. He confers sobriety, prudence, good sense, dependability, and patience . . . Saturn is the Lord of Time; but if you have built the foundation, walls, and roof secure, then Saturn will do you little harm."

Saturn is the ruler of the sign of Capricorn, the natural tenth house of the zodiac. It is said to be the planet of love of tradition and opposition to change.

No, the readings say: Saturn *rules change!*

> In Saturn we find the sudden or violent changes— those influences and environs that do not grow, as it were, but are sudden by that change of circumstances materially, or by activities apparently upon the part of others that become a part of self in the very associations. And yet these are testing periods of thy endurance, of thy patience, of thy love of truth, harmony and the spirit that faileth not.
>
> From the combination of this with Uranus we find the extremes; the environs materially or mentally in which the very opposites may be expected. Remember, only in Christ Jesus do extremes meet. 1981-1

Those who recognize in themselves the tendency to start a lot of projects in which they lose interest and seldom finish will find this excerpt interesting.

From Saturn we find the tendency for the starting of new experiences . . . new associations . . . and
unless these are tempered with mental influences
they are rarely carried to their full termination. This
again would be as a warning . . . When thou hast
chosen that direction, that activity thou would take,
know that thou art kept in a balance that is of the
material, mental and spiritual influences, near to
right. Then lay it not aside until it, the activity, has
borne fruit in thy mental and material experience.
361-4

The influences in Mars and Saturn show for urges
that will develop towards those things pertaining to
music. [The entity entered from Venus] . . . continually starting this or that activity which has to do or
deals with new associations, new relations, new activities . . . of not only self but those about the entity.
324-5

There are dozens of extracts stating specifically that
Saturn rules *changes,* and we will quote several to rein-
force this point:

We find in Saturn many changes in the experience. The entity will ever find itself very opposed to
being poor, and would go to almost any length to
obtain the material things of life. Let not these, thy
good works, be evil-spoken of, because of material
things being considered to such a degree as to dis-
regard others' privileges or obligations . . . 3205-1

In Saturn we find the inclinations for changes, as
to this, that or the other; and to muddle a great
many things together in the activity.
Hence that injunction as given by the sages of

old; "The merchant is never the student; neither is the student ever the merchant," should be a part of the entity's program in its choice of its activity in this experience. 1426-1

Astrologically we find that Venus, Saturn and Neptune are the urges. Thus these will be found to make many changes, yet the entity is one loving, a friend, one who may be counted on as a friend, or as a foe, to be sincere—if the directions are given properly for the entity during these trying periods. 3806-1

From the next reading we get an inkling of the tradition that Saturn is the great taskmaster, the teacher of patience under adversity:

In the astrological activities that produce . . . these experiences [desire for travel, desire for change] as innate, we find Uranus, Neptune, Saturn as ruling influences; which make for interest in yet the fear of occult and mystic forces. But rather [let it be] the expression of the *psychic*, rather than occult *or* mystic . . . [for] the greater development . . .

For in Uranus we find the extremes—and when the entity is very good, it's very, *very* good . . .

Those then of the experience must be tempered [by] the Venus influence.

While the Venus influences are latent, these should find the greater expression; else the urges from Saturn would make for the entity having *many* homes, or many marriages . . .

For consistency and persistency are sisters of patience; patience the entity needs to learn as its lesson in this experience. 1431-1

Saturn's Role in Soul Evolution

Besides giving the urge for changes in the earth plane, Saturn's role in the scheme of soul evolution is one of sorrow and change. To put it another way: the need for changes sends the soul or attracts the soul to Saturn after an earth life in which too many of God's laws have been misused:

(Q) What is meant by banishment of a soul from its Maker?

(A) . . . as given in the beginning to choose for self as in the earthly plane, all insufficient matter is cast unto Saturn. To work out his own salvation as would be termed in the word, the entity or individual banishes itself, or its soul, which is the entity . . . 3744-3

In the spheres of many of the planets within the same solar system, we find they [the entities] are banished to certain conditions in developing about the spheres from which they pass, and again and again and again return from one to another until they are prepared to meet the everlasting Creator of our entire Universe, of which our system is only a very small part.

. . . for it is self, and selfishness, that would damn the individual soul unto one or the other of those forces that bring about the change that must be in those that willfully wrong his Maker. It is not that which man does or leaves undone, but rather that indifference toward the creation [other creatures] that makes or loses for the individual entity. Then, let's be up and doing . . . 3744-4

Finally, to summarize Saturn's function of remolding or reclamation, the following reading compares Saturn with the Earth:

For the earth and Saturn are opposites, as it were
. . . to Saturn go those who would renew or begin
again, or who have blotted from their experience
much that may be set in motion again through
other influences and environs that have been a portion of the entity's experience. 945-1

The sex glands are associated with Saturn, according
to the readings.

URANUS

There is less variation between astrology textbooks
and the readings in the meaning of Uranus.

One of the astrology magazines says that Uranus is
concerned with occultism, originality, altruism, change,
independence; the metal, uranium; the ankles, as part
of the body; and ruler of the sign Aquarius.

McCaffery says: "Uranus is peculiarly the planet of insight into the laws of nature. This insight seems to come
in flashes, which reveal just how and when material things
can be made more useful. It is the planet of the inventor,
and is original and scientific, almost never emotional . . .
Uranus is the planet of electricity. It is sometimes said to
be malefic, for when it strikes, it can cause the whole efforts of a lifetime to tumble down and be destroyed. This
is usually because the plan of life has been wrong. The
old has to be destroyed before something new can enter
. . . It is sometimes said to be the planet of revolutionar-
ies, for it is never content to allow old institutions to continue without change. For this reason Saturn and Uranus
are ever in mortal conflict . . ." (pp. 77-78)

The key word for the meaning of Uranus, in the readings, is *extremes,* as the reader will have noted from allusions to it in the Saturn section. It is also the planet of
occultism, as distinct from psychic; which means "of the
soul, spiritual," according to the readings. Textbooks

state that Uranus is very likely the higher octave of Mercury, just as Neptune is the higher octave of Venus. The readings state that Uranus, in the human glandular system, refers to the thyroid, the will. Textbooks and the readings are not too far apart in their understanding of Uranus; but as usual the readings seem to add a deeper meaning to the concept of Uranus's role.

Here are some extracts, culled from dozens, on Uranus's extremism:

> From Uranian influences we find the extremist. And these tendencies . . . will develop especially through the early teen age years, when there will be moods and . . . wonderments . . . These [Uranian tendencies] make for also the intuitive influences and the abilities for the development in the very psychic forces of the entity. 1206-3

> In the urges from astrological aspects we find Mercury, Uranus, Venus and Jupiter as the influences through which the entity has received an awareness.
> One of the high mental ability, yet one very extreme in many ways.
> Oft . . . too easily discouraged. Hence . . . it will require that the entity set a purpose and a goal, and be not deterred from same . . . 2572-1

> Those of exceptional abilities with Uranian influence may be *well* said also to mean exceptional abilities to err, or to be led astray in the direction not best for . . . self's development. 38-1

> In Uranus we find the extremes, and the interest in the occult—the mystical. This is well, if it is balanced in the spiritual nature . . . 2571-1

. . . in benevolent influences in Mars and Uranus [both in Libra, sign of balance], these bring for the exceptional abilities as respecting intuitive forces for the body, and as for the abilities . . . to quiet those who would show wrath, or any unkindly feelings toward another. Oft will the entity—if trained especially in this formative period—be able to act as oil upon troubled waters, as that inter-between which will make for beauty in the lives of those the entity contacts, making for a bond of sympathy, of union, that will be exceptional . . . as well as . . . awakening of abilities within self . . . that may be the peacemaker, not only among individuals, but in groups, in classes, in states, in masses. [Entity entered from Jupiter, with Venus, Mars, and Uranus also influencing.] 1911-1

This entity, we find, took its flight, or position, from the planet of Uranus, with Venus and Mercury controlling the destiny in the present earth plane. Hence the necessity of the entity's training, especially, in those elements having to do with purity in love and affection, and of nobleness and goodness . . . that come with that mode of expressing itself . . . for with the entity under these influences, with the exceptional conditions as come from influences of Uranus, we find that the entity's manifestations in the present plane will be exceptionally good or very bad. 143-1

[The entity] is not only a Uranian but an Atlantean, and the combination will be something to *deal with!* as to temper, as to having its way; for it *will* have its way, irrespective, for the first fourteen years . . .

As for the aspects in the Uranian influence, we find the extremes. The entity will be at times very

beautiful in character—at others very ugly; very
beautiful in body and mind—at others the other
extreme. For these have an influence, and the entity will be an extremist through the first fourteen
years of its experience.

High mental abilities. One that will make a study
of how to have its way . . . *do not* break the will . . .
rather give the lesson by precept and example.
1958-1

In the Uranian influence . . . the extremes . . . For
there will be periods, natural to a Uranian, when for
a few hours or a few minutes or a few days it will be
very, very morose . . . These will arise . . . out of nowhere . . . 2005-1

Some readers will get a clue, here at least, as to why
they may have sudden and extreme moods which seem
to descend from nowhere. Uranus is probably one of the
planets under whose influence their entry was made
into the earth plane. See the last sentence of the previous reading, and also the following:

Astrological, then, we find the entity coming under the influence of Mercury, Jupiter, Saturn, Venus
and Uranus . . .
In . . . the Uranian [influences] . . . periods when
there seems to be every condition imaginable
awry—whether business relations, social relations,
financial conditions—*every* condition seems awry.
Again there are seasons of, most things come too
easy. 5-2

In Uranus we find the extremes. Thus the entity
in spiritual, in mental and in material things finds
periods when it is as to the mountaintops and again

in the depths of despair. 3706-2

The following excerpt indicates that Uranus combined with Mercury accounts for garrulity.

> Easily might the entity become one that would talk of self too much.
>
> While the entity will ever be a good listener, do direct the entity so that there is always the consideration for others.
>
> Astrologically—we find Uranus (the extremist, of course, in same), Mercury (the high mental abilities; for at least eight to ten experiences . . .). 2922-1

In a reading on the evolution of the soul, we find that after the soul has gone to Saturn for reclamation, the return can be, or perhaps must be, through Uranus. Here are portions of the reading:

> . . . know that every thought and act, is that being builded . . . in their sojourns in the spheres—make for this entering in. As in earth . . . matter takes all its various forms of presentation of . . . energy, *or* force, as radiated from the various effects of this solar aspect . . . all force in *this* [earth] sphere taking on that appearance . . . known as threefold, or the aspects of a threefold nature. As in Jupiter—taking on those ennobling forces, whether they be from earth, from Venus, from Mercury, from Mars . . . As in Saturn—that [sphere] to whom all insufficient matter is cast from its remolding . . . either re-entering through those of the Uranian—which makes for the accentuations of very good or very bad, and making, in their relationships . . . for *extraordinary* conditions; taking on those forces known in earth's

plane as from occult influences. 311-2

The Law of Balance

When the influences of Saturn and Uranus are part of the planetary urges of an individual, it seems logical to assume that such an individual has a special lesson to learn about applying the spiritual Law of Balance. Torn between the urges to extremes from Uranian sojourns, and the changes constantly presenting themselves, both inwardly and outwardly, from Saturn's influence, the individual would find himself or herself in a constant state of flux. This might force the will to make decisions about balance between the extremes. Several readings seem to be pointing up such a need.

> We find in Uranus the extremes, because of an *inner* feeling; not merely because of the age of changes . . . in the material environs of the entity. For, we find periods when apparently without reason outwardly there is over enjoyment . . . and then others when it becomes rather the recluse, or morose, or . . . inclined to sulk, as called by some . . .
>
> Make thy life . . . the well-rounded life; preparing self for the home rather than for a career. For, the greatest career of *any* individual is to make a home in such a . . . manner that each occupant—yea, each visitor to same—is better for having known and come into contact with the entity. 2443-1

The person for whom the following reading was given entered from Uranus, with six additional planets influencing the mental urges (irrespective of will). One of the six is Neptune, next to be discussed. Yet we find this admonition to keep the balance:

. . . and while the mental body may be termed the *exceptional* in mental abilities, these should be guided in the proper channels and kept as of a *unit* of the whole expression; knowing that to sidetrack, to accentuate, any one portion of experiences in the mental or physical forces of the body is to prevent the well rounded development as is necessary for . . . development in the material plane . . .
Keep thine heart pure, thine body strong, thine mind open. Attune thy inner man to the harps and the chords of the Universe, and harken to the love that brings service—service—to all. 1735-2

Uranus in the glandular system is represented by the thyroid, the will.

NEPTUNE

Neptune is the sixth planet outward from the Earth, counting Earth as number one. We find that the textbooks and readings agree in assigning mysticism and love of the sea to Neptune. Neptune is supposed to be the higher octave of Venus and is also associated with the arts. One magazine says that Neptune symbolizes compassion, the cinema, dreams, esthetic interests, liquor, gases, vapors, odors.

McCaffery states that Neptune, like Venus, rules music; that it gives second sight and the gift of prophecy; it is diffuse, elusive, emotional, and mystical. "Neptune makes mystics, whereas Uranus makes occultists . . . Neptune's vibrations can give the composer in one moment the whole of an opera. It will depend upon the rest of the chart whether this will be written in musical score, for Neptune of itself does not contribute any love of active hard work. The Neptunian inclines to be the dreamer."

We cite a few extracts from the readings which illustrate these points:

. . . the soul and spirit took its flight . . . from that far away force as exercised in Neptune. Hence we have an entity that . . . will be peculiar to other people, rarely ever being understood; yet one with the spiritual insight of the developing in [the] earth plane, and one whom others would be, could be, benefited by, by being in contact with this entity. 2553-8

For the extremes of Uranus as well as Neptune are a portion of the entity's experience . . .

From Neptune we find that being close to waters, on waters, or about waters, is very well . . . and this also gives those abilities as the mystic—the interest in the unusual, as in the abilities of seeing, feeling, experiencing that which to most would be the unseen forces about the entity.

These are well to be cultivated, not abused, not encouraged by giving thought to what the reaction should be, but keep the spiritual import, the spiritual necessity—which has been a portion of the entity's experience through one of its sojourns, as one who accepted the veil. 2308-1

Neptune *and* Uranus make for an interest in reading matter that is of unusual nature. Things that pertain to mysteries, or conditions in individuals' or groups' lives that are unusual, the uncanny and such . . .

And, for the better development of the entity, as it develops or progresses through the experiences of this sojourn, the dwelling near large bodies of water, or upon large bodies of water, will be the natural elements for the development; giving rise to the abilities both in the occult and in the mystic influences. 406-1

The following excerpt indicates that the soul entered from Neptune, with Uranus, Jupiter, and Mars influencing through the tendencies:

> Hence the conditions as are exhibited in the present earth's plane in . . . love of the sea (see the body has gone to sea).
>
> In the influence, then, we find one of many exceptional abilities.
>
> One that is considered eccentric and peculiar, having many changeable moods.
>
> One loving mystery, and every condition as regards . . . a mystery of the sea, and of the sleuth or detective nature.
>
> One that should have been guided close in the study of those things pertaining to the mystery and the occult.
>
> One who will find the . . . greatest abilities in the present earth's plane in the study of the occult forces. 2213-1

> In Neptune we find the inclinations for things that have to do with water and over water and to be on waters . . . These then give an urge again, as through Saturn, for change of scene and change of environment—and the desire for travel . . . those things that are exciting . . . that pertain to the heroic and hero worship. This urge must ever be tempered, then, with directing the entity to the character of ideals . . . 1426-1

In the following, the entity entered from Neptune, which in the natal chart is located at 10 Virgo. According to orthodox astrology, a watery planet in an earth sign is more or less at home, although Neptune is positioned in a sign opposite the one it is supposed to rule, Pisces. All this is interesting in view of the reading.

> Here we find unusual conditions, especially owing to the long periods of interims between material sojourns. And thus . . . one that oft appears to be lost in confusions of itself; being highly sensitive to those influences from without.
>
> Thus . . . an entity whose psychic abilities—if they are developed—may surpass much of that which has been the experience of many . . .
>
> Hence the needs for the study, the directing, the instructing of the entity in the sources of spiritual (not spiritualistic, but spiritual) influences . . .
>
> In the astrological aspects we find Neptune, Uranus, Venus and Saturn as the greater influence . . . Hence we will find the inclination for seeking the unusual places, strange conditions—taking up with and associating with strange surroundings, having strange playmates—the desire for [the] unusual in pets . . .
>
> From the Neptune influences—keep away from large bodies of water! These are opposite from much of that accredited as an influence from the astrological aspects of Neptune; though those things that come *from* and *over* large bodies of water . . . will be of a great interest to the entity; and the knowledge of same should be a part of the entity's experience. 2005-1

In the case of [4228] (see chart, p. 101), we find an interesting tie-in of Neptune with Arcturus, the greater Sun of our solar system. Please note that Mars and Septimus are afflicted; both are located in Cancer (if Septimus is Pluto, as we have reason to think). The language given here as to how the soul took its flight to Earth is unusual.

> We find the soul and spirit entity took its flight,

or its force being present and bringing this present entity's completeness, from . . Venus's forces, with those of Jupiter, Mercury, Neptune being the ones in the assistance to the conditions bringing the forces to this present plane's development, with afflictions of those in Mars and in that of Septimus. Arcturus being in the greater force for this development upon this plane, [the soul] receiving then the greater force by the influence of Arcturus, with . . . the dwelling forces of Neptune. The Moon's forces being those that have brought, and will bring, many of the influences from the forces of Venus . . .

As these, we find those inclinations:

With the strength of Jupiter forces, with that of Venus and Neptune . . . one given to letters, and of high exalted positions of self and all concerned therewith. Given to make show, or display, of that element that gives the greater expression of self. Hence, will must be directed, else with the influence of Venus's forces [it] would give detrimental elements in the life.

One whose forces from . . . Mercury will turn in the middle portion of life to those elements pertaining to the chemical forces, with that of Arcturus's forces giving strength to the elements [that are] directed in the entity. 4228-1

Neptune, in the body's glandular system, is represented by the cells of Leydig or lyden.

PLUTO
The planet Pluto was discovered in 1930, and even now there is some mystery and disagreement among astrologers in their interpretation of its meaning.

One astrology magazine says that Pluto opposes the conservative, and whatever is usual and accustomed.

According to this reference, Pluto opposes individualism and all forces tending toward individuals, in favor of mass movements, with their race riots, and governmental tendencies toward socialism.

McCaffery is not so pessimistic. She says, in *Graphic Astrology,* that in most cases "Pluto merely throws people out of routine, so that adjustments have to be made. It is too early in the study of Pluto to list all the matters under its control." She disagrees that Pluto rules dictators, for dictatorship has existed from remote centuries, and Uranus is more dictatorial than Pluto. She suggests that Pluto has some rule over Scorpio and also has rule over Aries. Research on Pluto is continuing. McCaffery states in another of her books, *Astrology: Its History and Influence in the Western World* (Scribners, New York, N.Y., 1942), "My own finding is that it rules change . . . a change that marks the end of an old condition and the beginning of a new. The changes brought about by Pluto, however, are not the sudden dynamic changes such as are brought about by Uranus. In fact they are often unappreciable for a long period, but they are definite ones."

As we have previously mentioned, the readings indicate that Saturn rules changes, and Uranus, extremes. Impulses from either are testing periods for the soul-entity and can be considered good or bad according to the way in which you view schooling or hard lessons. In this sense, if Pluto means a shifting of routines and mass movements that negate the individual, Pluto must be considered a "malefic" by orthodox astrological standards.

We prefer the word *regeneration* with reference to Pluto, since it is a higher-octave planet, as are Uranus and Neptune. In this case, *regeneration* means a higher consciousness and closer to the ideal, the Christ Consciousness. There is some evidence for this in the Edgar

Cayce readings. But first let us consider the names themselves.

Pluto is the seventh planet outward from the Earth, and prior to its discovery in 1930 the readings mentioned a planet *Septimus,* Latin for *seventh.* Later readings mentioned Pluto by name, and 826-8 gave the categorical statement that Pluto and the legendary *Vulcan* were one and the same.

Septimus is mentioned more often in the readings than are Pluto and Vulcan. The actual meanings of the urges from Septimus are unclear and fragmentary, and the meanings are usually those of an "afflicted" planet.

> Astrologically we find most all, in varied spheres, reacting through the soul-consciousness of the entity; Mercury, Pluto, Mars, Venus, Jupiter, Saturn, Neptune. All of these in various manners.
>
> Sudden changes are indicated in Saturn; high mental ability and capabilities in Mercury; *self-centeredness* in Pluto, and earthward in the application of self. [Pluto is in Gemini; author's italics.]
>
> In Venus we find the attraction to and from the opposite sex; in Jupiter a universal consciousness; in Neptune an interest in psychological and spiritual things.
>
> We find in Mars a high, exalted opinion of self; which is well, but abused—as it may be in Pluto, or in Mercury—may become a stumbling stone rather than a stepping-stone to advancement in this present sojourn. 3126-1

One of the first life readings given by Mr. Cayce (November 16, 1923, seven years before Pluto was discovered and named) mentions Septimus.

> In the relation to . . . the planets that [have], that

[are] and that will influence this body, we find the strongest of these at the moment of the birth . . . Venus and Neptune were the ruling forces for this body, with those of Mars in the 9th house, of Jupiter in the 12th house, of Uranus in the 7th house, see? Septimus almost at its zenith, yet not the ruling factor in this body's actions on this present plane, for with the position of Venus and Neptune this, the influence of Septimus, has become changed by the position of Pisces and the constellation of that of Castor and Apollo . . .

One well gifted towards the arts, especially in that of writing, or of composition, or of imagination, or of that that has to do with the finer things of life, as would be through the position [of] Castor, Apollo, Venus and Neptune.

One [who] should be nearer the great waters for its best development . . . will be well for this body to be wary of that of the influence of Septimus and the conjunction that will be within the next six months, else . . . accident, either through self or from the conditions of the trunk or the torso of the body . . . 583-1

Venus in the sunrise chart of this entity is placed at 6 Cancer, and within the next six months, or on May 18, Venus would conjoin natal Pluto at 9 Cancer.

In the influences that bring for warnings, as seen in Mars and Vulcan—beware of fire, and especially of firearms, or explosives . . . Beware of wrath in self, and in grudges as may be builded through wrath's influences in the relationships of the fellow man . . . Keep self attuned to that love force, even as in the occult influences. Beware of those . . . forces as make through chance . . . as of cabalistic or paleozoistic influences. 1735-2

Vulcan and the Dog Star (Sirius) are coupled in the following reading, and these are the influences attributed to them:

In astrological associations, these would appear adverse in their first appearance, coming much under the influence of the Dog Star and Vulcan. These make for that influence as has been of sudden changes in the social affairs, the relationships as respecting those of kinship, and those changes as respecting physical or business relations; yet these adversities may be used . . as stepping-stones for [the] soul's development, as well as of a mental and material change in the experience of the entity. As has been oft aptly quoted, it doesn't matter so much as to rebuffs as to the manner and the *use* same is put *to* in the experience of an individual . . . for in adversities *most* conditions grow, provided same is not of a nature to break the *will*, or to make for those conditions in which an entity reaches that position wherein it pities or belittles its own responsibilities, or its own individuality in the experiences through which it may pass. 1727-1

Septimus (Vulcan or Pluto) is not mentioned under the birth planets in the next reading, but a great deal of advice is given about the transiting planets. Under such advice comes the following:

. . . those that have to do with the afflictions of the body come under . . . the constellation of the Twins, or of Gemini, and that of the Great Bear. They will have to do with those of the digestion as afflicted by Septimus in those that come at two cycles especially in this entity. In that of February 1924, and in March 29 of same calendar year . . . beware

of conditions, and be careful of the diet during
those periods. [Pluto is at 3 in this natal chart.]
487-1

The most significant statement about Pluto's influence so far encountered in the readings is the following:

(Q) Just what are the effects of Pluto, in conjunction with one's ascendant?
(A) This as we find is entirely amiss from what we
might call a physical expression—but, as we find indicated, these [influences] are a development that
is occurring in the universe, or environs about the
earth—Pluto. Not as some have indicated that it is
gradually being dissipated. It is gradually *growing,*
and thus is one of those influences that are to be as
a demonstrative activity in the future affairs or developments of man towards the spiritual-minded
influences, or those influences outside of himself.
These [individuals] in the present, as might be
said, are merely [those] becoming *aware* of same.
Rather within the next hundred to two hundred
years there may be a great deal of influence [of
Pluto] upon the ascendancy of man; for it's closest
of those to the activities of the earth, to be sure, and
is a *developing* influence, and not one already established. 1100-27

What the expression "closest of those to the activities
of the earth" means, we can only guess. Coming to closer
influence? Most directly influencing the mind? Most po-
tentially spiritual influence of all the planetary "schools"
for learning outside the earth plane?
The evidence that this is so, and that Septimus is Pluto
and therefore spiritual consciousness, may be inferred
in the following reading, in which the development of

the Jesus soul as the perfect pattern is discussed.

In the developing, then, that the man may be one with the Father, necessary that the soul pass, with its companion the will, through all the various stages of development, until the will is lost in Him and he becomes one with the Father.

In the illustration of this, we find in the man as called Jesus. In this: This man, as man, makes the will the will of the Father, then becoming one with the Father and the model for man . . .

When the soul reached that development in which it reached earth's plane, it became in the flesh the model, as it had reached through the developments in those spheres, or planets, known in the earth's plane, obtaining then One in All.

As in Mercury pertaining of Mind.

In Mars of Madness.

In Earth as of Flesh.

In Venus as Love.

In Jupiter as Strength.

In Saturn as the beginning of earthly woes, that to which all insufficient matter is cast for the beginning.

In that of Uranus as of the Psychic.

In that of Neptune as of Mystic.

In Septimus [Pluto?] as of Consciousness.

In Arcturus as of the developing. 900-10

5

Cusps and the Zodiac

The readings place considerable emphasis on those who were born on the cusps, that is, the time when one zodiacal sign is ending and another beginning. Astrology textbooks simply say that such individuals partake of both signs in their characteristics. In all the readings studied by this writer, in which the individual is said to be born in or on the cusp, no mention is made as to which two signs are waning and increasing. For this reason we discuss the zodiac later.

We are left with a mystery. Why were not the signs called by name? Another mystery is that many persons born on the cusp were not designated as such. This may be because many other influences were at work and were similar to cusp influences.

Clearly, from the readings, a person born at such a time is and can be in a very difficult position.

> In entering the present experience, we find the entity is indeed one who may be said to be in the influence of . . . the cusps. While such influences are different, according to the information . . . given by many, we find that those who are near to the rising of one influence and the submerging—as it were— of another, are oft in those experiences where . . . they are in a strait, as it were, as to what should be the activity. 801-1

> In entering, astrologically, we find the entity coming under the influence of Uranus, Venus, Jupiter, and the cusps. In this [latter] relation . . . these in the physical life may be altered by the environmental conditions, and are changed by the will or directing influences in the present experience . . .
>
> Under Uranus—one exceptional in abilities, whether that of the mental or of physical endurance, or application of either.
>
> Under Venus—one loving in temperament, one that may be controlled by the influences as relate to sentiment, rather than . . . duty . . .
>
> In the influences in Jupiter—these will bring strength and ennobling powers in the influence of the entity.
>
> Through the cusps, or that changeable influence in the variations as are experienced, felt or known as conscious innate feeling—these will *always* bring that of rebellion to others that would dominate. 220-1

In the above reading, for a child five years old, we have no accurate birth hours; but the solar chart for September 22, 1924, puts the Sun at 29 degrees Virgo; Uranus at 19 Pisces, Venus at 13 Leo, and Jupiter at 13 Sagittarius. No sign of the zodiac is mentioned as influencing the entity.

The individual next cited was born March 21, 1933; no birth hour is given. Solar chart puts the Sun at 29 Pisces. Uranus, Mercury, and Jupiter are given as influencing planets. There is no mention of the Piscean or Sun-sign influence.

This entity comes upon the cusps; thus we find at times conflicting emotions with the entity. During the formative period of mental and physical developments, we find that the entity may be easily led. 2411-1

The Piscean influence is mentioned in the reading for [282], born March 18, 1906, but not the Arian influence as might be supposed. The Sun is placed at 26 degrees, 58 Pisces.

In entering astrologically, we find the entity coming near the cusps and under the influence of Pisces—in its latter portion. Hence we will find, while the entity has altered much of that termed as astrological, these are as innate . . . conditions to be warned [about] concerning . . . the *physical* body. 282-2

Other "cusp-ers" are:

. . . with the abilities untrained [one] would bring those opposing forces as found in Saturn and the cusps. For in the cusps is seen, with those influ-

ences in the Uranian, that these bring those passions or those unruly conditions that may not be
subdued by force, but conquered, guided and led
in love. [Born March 17, 1913; Sun at 26 Pisces.] 960-
4

From the astrological aspects we find the entity
almost *exactly* upon the cusps. Hence we will find
two influences, and the entity oft needing, requir-
ing, a consideration by those making the choice of
environs for the entity during the early portion of
its developments . . . For there has been into this
keeping, in these beginnings, entrusted in this experience an entity that may mean as much to the
world as the entity meant to, means to, America.
[Born June 21, 1936; Sun at 29 Gemini.] 1208-1

In the astrological aspects we find the entity
coming very close to the cusps, or changes; yet the
more definitely decided influences the astrological
aspects may have . . . will be in the inclinations for
the entity to take himself so seriously, as he develops . . .
As the entity astrologically comes under the influences from the astrological sojourns—rather
than the astrological positions, we will find Venus,
Mercury, Mars and Uranus as a portion of the
entity's experiences . . . [Born February 18, 1938;
Sun at 28 Aquarius.] 1647-1

Not considered "cusp-ers," apparently, are: [305-1],
whose Sun is at 2 Cancer; [398-1], whose Sun is at 6 Cancer; [559-7] whose Sun is at 28 Taurus; [759-1], whose
Sun is at 26 Aquarius; [773-1], whose Sun is at 3 Taurus;
[1426-11], whose Sun is at 27 Gemini; [1635-3], whose
Sun is at 29 Gemini; and many others. The readings are

open to much more research in this area.

The Zodiac

It has already been hinted that the signs of the zodiac did not play an important role in most life readings. This is at variance with astrology textbooks which enumerate characteristics for each sign, and when an individual is born in Gemini, for instance, proceed to describe Geminians and ascribe characteristics to that individual according to the Sun sign. Even though the ascending degree is in a different sign, the inward characteristics, say the textbooks, conform to Gemini.

One key to this discrepancy, aside from the influences carried over from previous incarnations, may be found in reading 8-1 (born August 11, 1890; Sun at 18 Leo). The information is given that the physical birth took place late in the evening of August 11, and "In the early morn" (presumably, August 12) were "the soul and spirit forces completed."

We mention this in passing to illustrate the fact that, according to the readings, physical birth and soul birth were not always simultaneous. The reading then proceeds, not to describe the Sun in the Leo type of individual, but to say that the soul and spirit took their flight from Mercury, with the influence of Venus, Jupiter, and Uranus, with negative influences from Mars and Neptune. The next paragraph states:

> As to those [influences] of the constellations or of the zodiacal signs in the life of this entity, these are merely the wavering influences in the life, and not those directing forces ever present in the inner soul of this entity. These we find in opposition to much that is at present taught or given in [the] earth plane . . . 8-1

An explanation of why the planetary influences and previous lives' influences are all important at birth is given for [1796], born January 7, 1925. Following the descriptions of heredity and environment in their truest senses, the reading proceeds to put the zodiac in its proper relationship:

Thus we find this entity—as each entity—is in the present the result of that the entity has applied of creative influences or forces in every phase of its experience. Thus it makes for that called by some karma, by others racial hereditary forces.

And thus environment and hereditary forces (as are accepted) are in their reality the activities of the *mind* of the entity in its choices through the experiences in the material, in the mental, in the spiritual planes . . .

There are then those accredited signs or omens or indications of characteristics in the innate and manifested activities of the entity. But these are irrespective of what the entity is to do, or will do, respecting same.

In the interpreting of the records here, then, we find the entity from the astrological aspects is influenced not because of the position of the sun, the moon or of the earth in its relationships to planets or zodiacal signs or other influences. Yet all of these are recognized as part of the entity's environment. 1796-1

This entity's Sun is at 16 Capricorn. He is influenced by five planets, beginning with Mercury. He is influenced both by astrological and material sojourns, he was told. Although some people are influenced more by astrological or by material sojourns, a larger percentage are influenced by a combination of the two.

To restate the above, as put in another reading:

> Astrologically, then, we find the influences are
> not merely because of the position of a star or
> planet, sun or moon, or any of the astrological as-
> pects or effects or influences; but rather through the
> entity's activities these have an innate influence
> because of sojourns and activities of the innate or
> soul self through such environs . . .
> The material sojourns find expression more in
> the emotional portion of the entity's being . . .
> But from the astrological we find the influences
> innate, and some are to be cultivated, that may
> grow, that may expand, and become more a portion
> of the influence; just as others are to be curbed and
> a lesson gained and applied rather than allowing
> self to drift . . . 1700-1

For an individual who was born March 18, with the
Sun at 28 degrees of Pisces, but not designated as a
"cusp-er," we find a statement which certainly does not
clarify the importance of zodiacal signs.

> Hence the entity was born into the earth under
> what signs? Pisces, ye say. Yet astrologically from the
> records, these are some two signs off in thy reckon-
> ing. 5755-1

This discrepancy may be due to the precession of the
equinoxes, which is explained by Ellen McCaffery in
Graphic Astrology: "The vernal equinox is the day in
spring (about March 21) when day and night are equal
in time. Astrologically, the equinox falls on the day when
the Sun reaches the zero degree Aries. Our signs are thus
calculated from what is termed by astrologers the Aries
ingress, which . . . is now in the constellation Pisces, or
one sign behind."

About 2000 B.C. the signs and the constellations coincided, and March 21, or the vernal equinox, lay in the sign of the Ram or Aries. Now the signs and constellations are almost one sign apart.

One almanac says that the chart of the zodiac showing the human body surrounded by the symbols of the zodiac was first published about the year 1300. However, as years passed, the zodiac moved slowly backward along the path of the Sun, and the distance covered up to the present time is close to thirty degrees. This means that the sign of Aries now contains the constellation Pisces; the sign Taurus now contains the constellation Aries, etc. Astronomical observers, the almanac says, use the constellations. This can readily be interpreted from the signs by going backward one symbol.

Astronomers generally agree that it takes 26,000 years, approximately, for the Sun and its family of planets to revolve around the central Sun, Arcturus. This backward revolution is called the precession of the equinoxes. Thus, in 2,100 years, the backward movement puts the vernal equinox one sign behind.

Astronomers do not agree as to what degree of the sign of Pisces is now occupied by the Sun at the vernal equinox: 9 degrees is suggested by one, and 3 degrees by another, etc. At any rate, we are nearing the beginning degrees of the Piscean constellation and thus getting closer to the later degrees of the sign of Aquarius. It is conceded that Jesus of Nazareth lived and carried on His ministry in the early Piscean Age.

It is easy to see, then, that the statement about two signs off (for the March 18 individual) is partially explained. According to hints and statements in the Cayce life readings, as this writer interprets them, the error of an additional sign off may be explained by erroneous adjustments of calendars The Persian calendar and the zodiacal signs are supposed to be the most accurate.

In life reading 2011-3, the entity was very much interested in astrology and was told that this stemmed from an experience in Egypt.

> . . . the entity was put in command of the preparations for the associations in the land of Saad and the Golden City, and the Mongoloid land. For to these three the entity was sent to act as an interpreter of the various astrological conditions that were to be drawn [up] by the various groups . . . The interests of the entity in those pertaining to astrology arise from that sojourn, also [things] pertaining to buildings, geometrical signs, symbols, pictures, things that illustrate . . . For the Egyptian and the Persian records are quite varied [at variance]. If the entity would study astrology, do not put the signs in the Egyptian calendar but in the Persian, for the Persian interpretations are more proficient than the Egyptian. This is not belittling the efforts of the entity nor of the Egyptians in those periods, but the variations in time have been corrected by the Persians and not by the Egyptians. The Egyptian calculations are thirty degrees off [one sign]. 2011-3

Although we have a possible explanation for the second of the "two signs off," it would take an expert in the subject of ancient calendars with all their discrepancies to explain what this means in terms of the Sun in the zodiac, in the present.

There are other references in the readings to the Persian calendar. One of these is from 826-8, and we include part of the reading leading up to this because it discusses the matter of which chart should be used for an individual—the physical birth or the soul birth.

(Q) Should an astrological horoscope be based

on the time of physical birth or the time of soul birth?

(A) On time of physical birth; for these are merely *inclinations,* and because of inclinations are not the influence of will. *Will* is that factor of the spiritual forces or the gift, as it were, *to* man . . . as he came into material form, with which choice is made, see? Hence if astrological aspects are to be assumed, then physical. But these make for oft confusing experiences to those casting such charts and reading from that which has been the version [interpretation] of same.

For as we have indicated, there are two, yea three phases or schools through which such information, such charts, such characters have been carried— the Egyptian, the Persian, the Indian.

The Persian is a combination and the *older* of all of these, and these are as logos [?], or as charts that have been set. That they have become as experiences in the activities of individuals, to be sure, is not disputed; but the world does not govern *man, man* governs the world! And the inclinations astrologically show whether man has or has not applied will!

Then the inclinations are good, but they may be stumbling-stones if one submerges will to listen at inclinations! 826-8

A reference to our misinterpretation of the zodiac and to the precession of the equinoxes comes in reading 311-2. This whole reading is worth study, for it touches upon so many puzzling subjects.

. . . the *solar* system is also passing through its various spheres, that are being acted upon by the forces *from* without, or that as is ordinarily known—

or has been *determined* and named, though not
rightly, or wholly rightly in their aspects—as those
forms in the various *months* . . . yet we find a *simi-
larity* of expression, rather than action. *Action* from
the *motive* forces *from* the entity's *experience* or development, or through either the *earth's* experience
or the spheres about same. 311-2

The whole purpose of each life reading given by Mr.
Cayce was to be helpful to the individual.

In giving that which may be helpful to this entity
in the present experience, respecting the sojourns
in the earth, it is well that the planetary or astrological aspects also be given. It should be understood, then, that the sojourning of the soul in that
environ [planetary], rather than the position [square,
trine, etc., or planets at birth], makes for the greater
influence in the experience of an entity or body in
any given plane. This is not belittling that which has
been the study of the ancients, but rather it is giving the *understanding* of same. And, as we have
indicated, it is not so much that an entity is influenced
because the Moon is in Aquarius or the Sun in Capricorn or Venus or Mercury in that or the other
house, sign, or the Moon and Sun sign, in that one
of the planets is in this or that position in the heavens; but rather because those positions in the heavens are from the *entity* having been in that sojourn
as a soul! This is how the planets have the greater
influence in the earth upon the entity, see? For the
application of an experience is what makes for the
development of a body, a mind, *or* a soul. 630-2

In summary, the writer believes that the constellations, as well as zodiacal signs, are important in inter-

pretations of astrological charts. The life readings are replete with references to Arcturus, the Greater Sun, and the way out of this particular solar system, along with Septimus; with references to the Pleiades, Dog Star, Orion, the Great Bear, Polaris, and others.

It should not be concluded that the life readings never include descriptions of the signs of the zodiac. The allusions are simply infrequent and seemingly of secondary importance. Here are a few which have been found.

For [2668], born March 11, 1920, with the Sun at 20 Pisces, no time of the day was given. A solar chart, putting the Sun on the ascendant as if at sunrise, also puts Uranus at 2 Pisces. This is the only mention of Pisces in the reading:

> In entering, we find astrologically the entity coming under the influences in Pisces, in Venus, in Mercury, Jupiter and Uranus. 2668-1

In 276-2, again we have no accurate birth time, and only that the entity was born January 15, 1918. A solar chart shows nothing occupying the sign of Aries, yet the reading states:

> In entering, we find the influences astrologically in Aries—which will require in the present experience the use of the mental abilities of the entity in making its choice. Hence . . . through the formative period of the mental developments being especially susceptible . . . 276-2

On August 26, 1913, [641] was born, and the solar chart puts his Sun at 2 Virgo. The sign of Virgo is otherwise unoccupied. The reading states:

> In the present experience we find more of those

conditions as latent urges than those as have been manifested or expressed through the application of will . . .

In entering the earth's plane, we find the entity coming under the influence of Jupiter, Mercury, Venus, and the benevolent influences in [the] Sun and in Orion. 641-1

The three stars in Orion are Betelgeuse at 27 Gemini; Bellatrix at 19.50 Gemini, and Rigel at 15 Gemini. This individual has Mars, Saturn, and Pluto in Gemini but none of the three is mentioned as influential planets.

We have both Pisces and Leo mentioned in 2905-3, for which we have only a solar chart. The Moon is in Leo, but is not mentioned as influential; Mercury is in Pisces, but is mentioned fourth in importance.

Astrologically we find urges, not because the Moon or the Sun or Leo or Pisces may have been in this or that position when the entity was born. But the entity as a consciousness experienced those activities or awarenesses in those environs. Thus these become part of the soul experience. As will be found, Leo—or the consciousness of that mind will be a part of the entity's awareness. Thus at times the entity will appear headstrong, willful . . . 2905-3

Again, in a solar chart for [406], born January 16, 1919, the four important planets are Mars, Uranus, Jupiter, and Neptune. The reading states:

Through Aries associations, there are the abilities of a high *mental* development; yet there are rather those warnings for this entity regarding accidents to the head. Injuries of some nature may come . . . either during the next four months or early portion of '34. These warnings are from influences that come from Aries or head associations with Mars.

Hence, as to the greater astrological activities from sojourns in environs, Uranus is the greater influence for the present experience. 406-1

No planet occupies the sign of Aries, although Aries may be the ascendant in a correct birth chart, with the time of day known. Mars itself is at 21 Aquarius.

We have a correct birth chart for [1710], born February 26, 1915, near Norfolk, at 6 p.m. (5:56 p.m. local time; 11:00 p.m. Greenwich mean time). Piscean influence is described (Sun is in Pisces) and also the influence of Libra, for which we can find no reason unless Venus, the first planet mentioned, carries the Libran influence. Mercury and Uranus are the other two planets mentioned. Note the positions of Venus, Mercury, and Uranus, none of which are "rising" or near the zenith or ascendant. (See Figure 6, p. 111.)

We quote significant excerpts from this reading:

There have been periods when the entity apparently has been blocked in the preparation for this or that activity, this or that association with individuals, and circumstances that would have changed or do change the whole course of events for the entity.

These influences all come from the Atlantean's activities that have brought Libra (of the balance) into force in such a manner that it might be said of the entity, indeed there is a path cut out for thee— the gods have directed that ye will have the opportunity to show forth thy worth . . .

In the astrological aspects we find the Piscean influence.

Hence we find the entity apparently oft bearing

the brunt of others' misapplication of time or of purpose, or even of material things. But know that such only offers an opportunity for self for greater development in every phase of the experience. Not that these are to always be, but they are as examples of the fact that whom the Lord loveth He *calleth,* and *prepareth* through chastenings, through trials, through those experiences which will develop one for the activities in which greater successes of every nature may come.

For thy talents being many, much will be—is—required of thee.

Kick not against circumstance, that has apparently at times fraughted thee in thy efforts—whether they have been thy social relationships with those of the opposite sex, or whether in the apparent manner of preparation for activities in chosen fields of service in the material world. But know that these have been and are opportunities for *greater* advancement.

In Venus as combined with Mercury, *and* the activities in Uranus, we find the interests in things mechanical as well as those that require the application of such by the material hands . . .

As to the application of self respecting the astrological forces—these as we find are only urges. As to what one does *with* and about same depends upon choices made.

Hence the needs for each soul, each entity to have a standard, an ideal by which the patterns of the life, or its associations with its fellow man, may be drawn . . . 1710-3

We cannot recognize the orthodox description of Libra from the above, nor reconcile its influence, unless Libra is on the ascendant and we are at least one sign behind! If we are two signs behind and Scorpio is on the ascendant, then Venus, the most influential planet, is just barely rising.

The above might be said to be a good description of Pisces.

6

Planets, Transits, and Cycles

Only occasionally, in the life readings, was the accurate birth time given, corrected, or verified. By accurate birth time is meant not just the place, the month, day of the month, and year, but the time of the day or night, to the minute. Only with the latter information can a correct horoscope be erected, giving the sign and degree at the eastern or ascending point, together with the correct north, south, and west. Then the cusps of the other houses may be put in position.

With the correct information given in approximately forty-five readings (there may be more, as further research uncovers them), accurate charts have been erected by three competent astrologers. Two of these were professionals not connected with the A.R.E., and one is a member.

At the beginning of this book it was stated that 150 readings for children formed the chief basis of our intensive study. Here is an interesting breakdown of the number of planets which influenced these youngsters:

In only one reading was just one planet mentioned, the one from which the soul took flight.

In four readings, two planets were given as influential.

In twenty-seven readings, three planets were given.

In fifty-two readings, four planets were given.

In twenty-four readings, five planets were given.

In eight readings, six planets were given.

In four readings, seven planets were given.

In one reading, eight planets were given.

The total of these is 121; leaving twenty-nine children's readings in which only Earth lives were influential, or in which readings were for very young babies and descriptions but not names of planets were mentioned, and physical warnings about the babies' health were given. Parents were sometimes advised to seek a life reading for the child later on.

It would appear from the above that most people have from four to six planets influencing their lives, and that among this number is the primary or most important one from which the soul took flight. In the readings, this planet is often mentioned first, and usually tallies with the life just preceding this incarnation; the second planet tallying with the life just preceding that one, etc.

In one answer from the 3744 series of readings, it is stated that not all the planets are effective in their influence upon an individual in the present life. The implication is that the entity has not sojourned in some of them recently enough to affect the present life; or the others are not involved particularly with the present planetary-earthly sojourn. Here is the key statement:

> The influence from any [planet] is from what
> planet that soul and spirit returns to bring the force
> to the earth individual, as it is breathed into the
> body, from whence did it come, that being the in-
> fluence. Not the revolution of the ideas as given
> from those who study of those forces . . . 3744-4

Later on in this same reading, it was asked if the tendencies of an individual are most influenced by the planets nearest the Earth at the time of birth. The answer was
that the individual is influenced most by the planet at,
or close to, the zenith when the individual soul took its
flight in coming to the earth plane. And the zenith, according to textbooks, is the midheaven or southernmost
point of the circle, farthest away from the person viewing the circle.

We have another clue to the primary planet in the following reading:

> The strongest power in the destiny of man is the
> Sun, first; then the closer planets, or those that are
> coming in ascendancy at the time of the birth of the
> individual; but let it be understood here, no action
> of any planet or any of the phases of the Sun, Moon,
> or any of the heavenly bodies surpass the rule of
> Man's individual will power—the power given by
> the Creator of man in the beginning, when he be-
> came a living soul, with the power of choosing for
> himself.
>
> The inclination of man is ruled by the planets
> under which he is born. In this far the destiny of
> man lies within the sphere or scope of the planets.
> With the given position of the Solar system at the
> time of the birth of an individual, it can be worked

out—that is, the inclinations and actions without will power taken into consideration. 254-2

The phrase "coming in ascendancy" means the three houses just below the ascendant, and the two houses just in front of the zenith or midheaven. At least, these meanings for zenith and ascending are the ones used in astrology textbooks. How can we be sure the readings used the terms with the same meanings? We cannot. Incidentally, astrology textbooks ascribe great importance to the ascendant, the zenith, and planets "rising" or on the left-hand side of the circle. The textbooks try to arrive at the most important planet or planets by various means: the ruler of the Sun sign, the ruler of the rising sign, the planets most "aspected," etc. Orthodox astrology does not say that all planets equally affect the individual or "native"; neither do the Edgar Cayce readings. To this extent there is agreement.

Transits and cycles are important factors in the individual horoscope, as given in the readings. By transits is meant the changes in position of the planets, Sun, and Moon from the birth date on. Here we come to the word *aspect*, so important in present-day astrologers' interpretation. As far as we can discover, these are the same as those defined in the textbooks: conjunction, square, opposition, trine, etc. If four planets are given as the influential ones in the reading, with Venus the one from which the soul took flight to Earth, for instance, any transiting aspect made by any planet to the natal four, or involving any of the natal four by their present positions, affect the individual.

If, for example, Saturn is not one of the natal four, but is presently squaring Venus, the birth planet, either in the heavens or squaring the natal position of Venus, then Venus will feel the effects of Saturn, the change-about-er! Whatever Venus means in the natal chart, whether it

is the love nature or an artistic talent, a changeover may
be due. Since all changeovers may be somewhat painful
or unsettling, the native, or individual, may feel frustrated and at sea.

On the subject of aspects, as such, it came as a considerable shock to this writer to discover that the natal planets are seldom or rarely in aspect to each other! If they
are, it seems almost accidental; and of all the aspects, we
have found that the conjunction is most often found. In
the natal chart, two planets may be conjunct, within one
to four degrees, and only one of the two be named as
one of the influential planets.

As to cycles and their influence upon the individual,
the readings indicate that approximately every seven
years there is a change and another cycle. There is some
evidence that seven years is not allotted to each of the
eight planets, that only the (say) four planets mentioned
as influential have seven years apiece and at the end of
the four cycles the first planet takes the fifth cycle, the
second planet the sixth, etc. This, of course, varies from
what is taught in traditional astrology.

> As to the appearances of the entity in the earth,
> and those influences that will bear upon the early
> experiences—we find that these, as may be seen,
> should be changed in the seventh and in the four-
> teenth year. These are as cycles of impressions and
> changes; and activities in the developing of the
> body, the mind, the soul . . . [Born December 8,
> 1938, at Detroit, Michigan, at 10:47 p.m.] 1788-3

> It will be seen, as we find from the records here,
> that varied experiences of the entity in its develop-
> ments through the [whole] cycle of its experience
> will be altered by the variation in the cycles of de-
> velopment; and that as may be given in the present

as having the greater influence will during its seventh to fourteenth or fifteenth year be changed—as when it is twenty-one and twenty-eight; and *then* it will be determined as to whether it is to be the material or the mental and spiritual success to which this entity may make for its experiences in the present sojourn. [Born August 31, 1936; no planets given.] 1332-1

As to the appearances in the earth, not all of these may be given. For these ye attain in thy varied cycles of unfoldment. [Born February 19, 1932; no planets given.] 3053-3

As there was in the entering of the entity's inner forces into this physical body, the first [change] will come at the age of seven, then at fourteen, at twenty-two—these will be decided changes, or one will so lap over the other—but may be said to be periods when changes will come to this entity; for there was some lapse of time (as time is counted from the material) between the physical birth and the spiritual birth. 566-1

As to the appearances in the earth, these have been quite varied. Not all may be given in the present, for with each cycle there comes another experience as a part of the entity's problems or help. Just as some set that each day or each hour, as the earth passes from phase to phase of the constellations or the signs of the zodiac, there comes greater impression. Rather is it as [the influence of] the cycles. For it is admitted that the body changes completely each seven years. 3637-1

We have in reading 405-1 a reference to the "second

cycle of Jupiter's influence, which begins in 1940." This child of eleven years of age was born March 2, 1922. She entered from Jupiter, according to the reading, with "Mercury and Venus, with Mars" as influential planets. The reading makes it clear that Jupiter affects the whole sojourn and is emphasized by cycles: "Then, Jupiter being the ruling influence . . . from the astrological aspects, as the time of birth, as well as to the sojourn of the entity . . . "

Doing a little figuring, it can be seen that from 1922, the birth year, to 1940, the time of Jupiter's second cycle, there is a span of eighteen years. Up to seven years of age the child was under a Mercury-Jupiter influence; up to fourteen years, under a Venus-Jupiter cycle, ending in 1932 or 1933. Then from fourteen to twenty-one years of age, came a cycle of Mars-Jupiter, which brings us to 1939 or 1940, when the reading states that Jupiter's second cycle begins. This is a piece of evidence that the cycles make the rounds of the influential planets, over and over again.

A Different Kind of Cycle

The quotation from this reading speaks for itself:

> . . . we find in this particular entity, *and oft,* ones that enter an experience as a *complete cycle,* that is, upon the same period under the same astrological experiences as in the sojourn just before (that is, being born upon the same day of month—though time may have been altered); find periods of activity that will be very much the same as those manifested in the previous sojourn, in the unfoldment and in the urges latent and manifested.

Psychology, philosophy, reasoning, dramatic art, the dramatic critic—these will be the character and the temperament that [are] to be dealt with [in this entity].

For, in the appearance before this, the entity entered as Jean Poquelin, known as Molière, the great French dramatist . . . [Author's italics] 2814-1

Molière was born January 15, 1622. This individual was born January 15, 1942.

We have a few other examples of such cycles. This person was born on October 2, 1940, and the reading stated:

Nickname the entity Franz . . . and there will be seen why . . .

Before this, the entity was in the Austrian or Hungarian land. There the entity was an unusual individual, in the name Liszt; being a composer as well as a musician. And as its activities through the experience were such as to make for certain characters of music, these in part will be of special interest to the entity in the present. The comparison may be easily seen . . . as to the faults, the failures, as well as the activities in which the entity then . . . rose to its place or position in the musical world.

That is why, then, the nickname Franz is suggested; for the entity was Franz Liszt. 2584-1

No accurate birth time was given, and there was no mention of planets. Musician Franz Liszt was born on October 22, 1811.

Patrick Henry was born on May 29, 1736; and this man, whose birth date was May 27, 1940, was described as Patrick Henry in the life just prior. We have the accurate birth time for [2294], as well as planets. He entered from Saturn.

From the astrological aspects we find the influences indicating the energetic activity of the mind as well as of the body.

Also there are the tendencies for extravagance, which should be curbed . . . through the early periods of its activity; for these will be a part of the inclinations, not only because of the Gemini influence but also the Saturn, Mercury, Jupiter, Mars and Venus influences.

As these planets were strong influences in the earth through the developing periods of . . . gestation, they will in the early portion of the life manifest the greater influence.

Hence we find one that will . . . show a general energetic activity . . . Not that there will not be affection, not that there will not be . . . preferences; but the very nature of the Gemini influence makes for the sudden changes of preferences, and the demonstrations in which there will be seen the influences of these . . . 2294-1

The birth chart for [2294] is on page 103. Beside each planet in the chart, we have indicated the order of mention, putting Saturn first, of course, as in the reading. The reading continued that the entity would have the ability to argue out everything; hence there should always be given the reason *why*, in its training.

As an orator the entity may be found to excel, as in its former experience; but this . . . will necessitate . . . training in those directions. For, as the awareness arises . . . we will find the entity inclined to shut self away at times, and at others to be *overactive* in giving expressions . . . For, in the developing years, there will be the tendency to seek liberty for its own self at any cost; and there should be given the whys, the causes, and the expression of the abilities that are reached through the Mercurian high mental experience, as well as the benevolent influences through the Uranian sojourn—so as to bring more and more the abilities to express for the universality of the activities . . . Hence the entity should be trained in *international law* . . . 2294-1

Notice from this chart that the number one planet, Saturn, is not the one closest to the zenith, or midheaven; nor to the ascendant. All the influential planets are on the left-hand side of the chart, or the rising side, or coming to ascendancy. The 12th house (just above the ascendant) is generally ignored as an important rising house by astrologers; yet in this chart, Mercury, the second most important planet, is just above the ascendant, in the 12th house.

This person, [2294], is not described as a Sun-in-Gemini type of person; however, Gemini influences him, presumably because Mercury (ruler of Gemini) is in Gemini and very close to the ascendant. Also presumably, the life just before this was ruled by Mercury primarily, and the reading says this was a "Mercurian high mental experience." This could, of course, mean in the environs of Mercury also. We do know that progress or soul evolution is made by application of lessons learned in planetary sojourns to the problems of earth life.

Summary

The text of this booklet contains only a small portion of the nearly 2,000 life readings that Edgar Cayce gave during his lifetime. The author has not attempted a complete survey of all the astrological references in the A.R.E. Library. What pertinent items still lie uncovered is a matter of deep interest to many of those concerned with astrology and the continuing work of the Association. Certainly a vast amount of material is available for further research and interpretation.

In closing, let the following reading (given February 14, 1924) continue the theme of universal soul forces, with planetary influences playing their usual accompanying role:

(Q) What are the laws governing relativity of all force?

(A) In giving the manifestation of such [a] law, which does exist, we first must consider that that is called force, and that force then in its relation, or the relativity of that force to all force.

There are, as were set in the beginning, as far as the concern is of this physical earth plane, those rules or laws in the relative force of those that govern the earth, and the beings of the earth plane, and also that same law governs the planets, stars, constellations, groups, that that constitutes the sphere, the space, in which the planet moves. These are of the one force, and we see the manifestation of the relation of one force with another in the many various phases as is shown, for in fact that which to the human mind exists, in fact does not exist, for it has been in past before it is to the human mind in existence.

In this, we see the law of the relations of conditions, space or time and its relation to human mind, as is capable of obtaining information upon the earth plane from a normal force or conditions. Hence, we bring the same word, relativity of force, to prove its own self, and condition, for we have as in this:

The earth in its motion, held in space by that force of attraction, or detraction, or gravitation, or lack of gravitation in its force, so those things that do appear to have reality, and their reality to the human mind, have in reality passed into past conditions before they have reached the mind, for with the earth's laws, and its relations to other spheres, has to man become a past condition. So it is reached only in the further forces as will show, and as is given, for man to understand in this developing, or this evolution from sphere to sphere, or from plane to plane, in this condition.

Hence, we find to the normal mind, there is no law as to relativity of force, save as the individual may apply same in the individual's needs of them. That is sufficient.

Then in a later paragraph the reading offered further insight and guidance to gaining of awareness in relationship with these universal forces.

The study from the human standpoint, of subconscious, subliminal, psychic, soul forces, is and should be the great study for the human family, for through self man will understand its Maker when it understands its relation to its Maker, and it will only understand that through itself, and that understanding is the knowledge as is given here in this state. 3744-5

Appendix I

Birth Charts and Examples of Life Readings

FIGURE 1
(see p. 64)

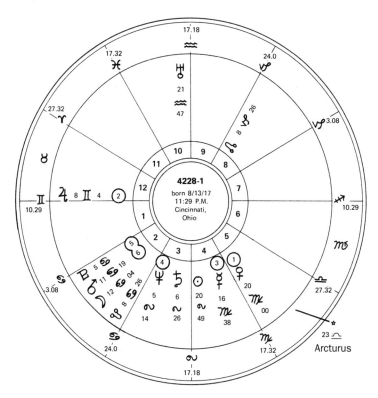

Example to Figure 3   Given 5-15-27
142-1   Male, 1 month   Born 4-4-27

(This is of special interest in light of warnings given about firearms, for an individual indicated to have been previously killed in a duel.)

In entering, we find the entity comes under the influence of Jupiter and Mercury with benevolent influences in Uranus and in Venus; hence we will find there will be many unusual conditions as will surround those influences as will be exhibited in the life of the entity. Yet as we find, there is also presented, through those cosmic influences and through the astrological conditions, those of the warnings as would be presented for the development of the mental, the physical and the spiritual influences as will become manifested through urges as will be exhibited in this body. Principally these have to do with those conditions regarding temper and the exercising of same as regards the will's influence. Not, then, that the will of the entity shall be broken but that same shall be guided in those directions that will bring the more benevolent and more powerful influence in the life through the Jupiterian influence.

Again we find that there will appear the square of those conditions between Mars and Uranus with Jupiter in the twelfth year in which the warning is especially against the relations of the entity as regarding firearms ...

There appears, as we see, the greater influence in Jupiter and in Mercury, with the benevolent influence in Uranus which becomes as exceptional conditions in the urges; being then very decided in the likes and dislikes, being inclined toward those conditions and positions of estate and of high mental

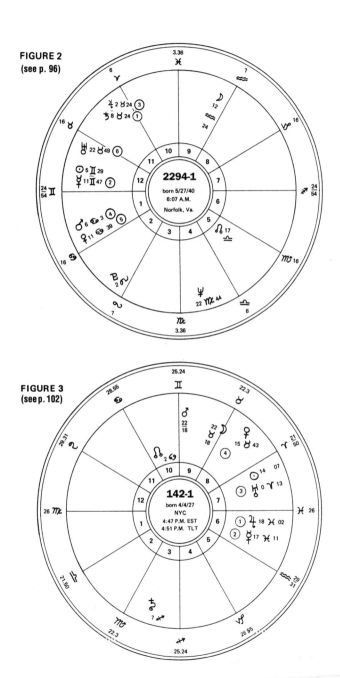

FIGURE 2
(see p. 96)

2294-1
born 5/27/40
6:07 A.M.
Norfolk, Va.

FIGURE 3
(see p. 102)

142-1
born 4/4/27
NYC
4:47 P.M. EST
4:51 P.M. TLT

and physical influence; inclined then toward aspiring to same through the abilities of the mental.

Hence the injunction as is given toward the direction of the will's influence in the life as respecting control of temper. For in this there may be brought those detrimental conditions especially as regarding the misapplication of station or position, rather than inclined towards those not of the plebeian but of those in the position of the leader. For the natural intent of the entity is toward that of the natural leader in the mental, in the social, in the political, in the financial forces of those who surround the entity.

Example to Figure 4   Given 12-13-32
398-1   Female, 2 years   Born 6-28-30

(For a child whose mother, a professional astrologer, saw in the child's chart danger of death in early childhood.)

In entering from the astrological and astronomical viewpoint . . . these would at some periods be very much in line with that ordinarily attributed to such—in *some* ways of judging same; while others are in almost opposition to that ordinarily adjudged as the astrological influence . . .

Coming under the influence of Neptune then, as we find, makes for the mystic forces in the experience of the entity; as liking and loving a mystery . . . So, one that has encompassed or covered the greater period in the developing of the individual entity or soul would be called the old, or the more highly evolved, or greater developed soul. This one will be unusual!

In the approaching of both Jupiter and Venus in their conjunction with the attributes of the triad [trine?], or the angle at which same comes to Uranus through the birth period of the entity . . . we find these not as the *influencing* in the experience of the entity, but as the relationships of those sojourns or planetary influences upon the dwellers upon the earth during this particular period they *influence* the life of the entity *by* their contributing to the impelling influences in the entity's experience . . .

So, with the directing through the period [of youth], know that these conditions arise from those influences that make for a *strong, well, healthy* physical body, and that the attributes are such that these may be led in that which becomes excessive in the forces of the mental only, or the spiritual-mental, or the carnal forces. As to these, those that direct must choose; hence the responsibility that comes upon those that would guide or direct.

With the tendencies in those influences from the sojourns . . . there comes those tendencies also wherein, unless these are developed into those channels where they come from the spiritual or the creative forces of the developing influences for the entity, not to be deceitful so much—but rather as one with the ability to *tweedle* [wheedle] . . . this, that or the other out of whatever source or channel it would try or attempt to do; and what is the life of a [wheedler]?

398-2   *(second reading for above)*   Given 8-31-33

Yes, we have the body, [398], and those conditions in the astrological aspects, especially in reference to those adverse influences that appear [imminent] in the experience of the entity in the near future; as well as that which has been builded by the entity in its sojourns through the spheres of activity where there is such a gathering of influences as to become active in a body-entity.

In giving that which may be understandable, and that which may be helpful from the material angle at this time, as we find, it would be well that all consider the varying aspects from that considered an astrological influence.

As we have given through these channels, astrological influences are effective in the experience of each and every entity. However, when the activities of a soul-entity have been such as to cause or to form the appearance of the entity in a particular sphere of [planetary] activity, the position of the sojourn of the entity *to* the earth *has* the greater influence than just the adverse or benevolent positions of the planet or of a whole solar system upon the *entity's* activity! . . .

Then, it is as this: When the activities of an entity, a soul in the earth, have been such that its passage from the earth would become a birth into the realm of matter known as Mars, Venus, Jupiter, Uranus, Neptune, Moon, Mercury, Polaris, or any of these that are effective in the universal influence, you see, the sojourn there *and* the position of the planets *are* more effective than the influence brought to bear because of a position in a certain place or portion of the universal forces, see?

Hence, as we find, these conditions are only as urges; or, as may be termed from some reasons or seasons of thought, the planetary influences from their positions are either benevolent, adverse or inter-between these activities—one drawing upon another; but the entity's *sojourn in* those environs makes the impulse for the mental activity, rather than the *position* of these!

Do we gather the variation?

Hence, for this particular entity at this time, as we find, there will be those conditions in which there will be seen adverse influences in the activity of the entity as related to the material sojourn of the body; but these will be rather in the form of *mental demonstrations* within the activity of the body, than purely mechanical-physical or physical-mechanical—whichever you would choose to term it!

Then, they will be *impulses*—and may be seen in the entity's experience particularly through this period, beginning with the fifth (5th) of September to the eighth or tenth (8th or 10th) of October, this present year.

As to what is to be done respecting such conditions, it would be well that all precautions known in the activity of the earth be taken (as particular attention to the activities of the body, and the hygienic influences in the experiences of the body) to avert an adverse influence in the health of the body itself. See?

Why? The question may be asked, why the mental hygiene, why the physical hygiene, particularly?

Because of those influences of the mental nature that would cause the body to be attracted to the character of influences that would be detrimental to the physical welfare or sojourn in the earth during that particular period!

It would be the same way that one might feel (this aside, of course) within self when awakening from a sleep, or from a revery, or from some mental urge to do or see or know something pertaining to something that apparently has nothing to do with the activities of the body-physical; as the mental desires to know of certain forces, forms, elements, or activities of elements, at that particular or immediate time. See?

Hence the same is active in this particular experience at this time of this body we are speaking of . . .

Example to Figure 5   Given 12-2-27
960-4   Male, 13 years   Born 3-17-13

(This reading, for a boy born deaf, indicated he had been involved in the French Revolution.)

This body is under the influences of Jupiter, Mercury, and Uranus with those [afflictions] in Saturn. As to these influences as are seen, irrespective of the application of will's forces we find . . .

The inability of the entity to understand why that ego should be subjugated to another. Hence with these complicating conditions in the present plane, we find much care, much attention should be given in that stage when the mind and [the] reactions from same will give that correct balance with same, that the entity may develop [toward] that oneness of purpose.

In the universal forces found in the astrological conditions and positions, irrespective of the will, we find one that has innate high and noble purposes. He is often misunderstood, and when rebuked, the entity little understands why . . .

One that is high-tempered, yet, guided in the correct way and manner, will bring much joy, much happiness, much of better understanding to those that would be found in oppression, and one that would bring release to many.

FIGURE 4
(see p. 104)

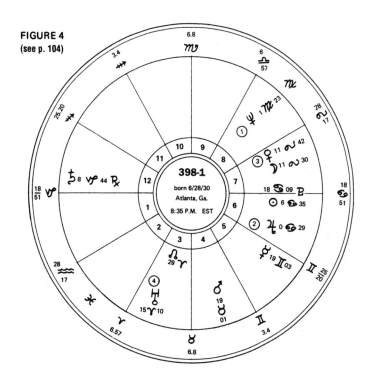

He should be a lawyer. One that will bring through those abilities, guided aright, those conditions of the more . . . knowledge of that unison, of the purpose in *right for right's sake,* and not because another says this is right or wrong . . .

One that with the abilities untrained would bring those opposing forces as found in Saturn and the cusps. For in the cusps is seen, with those influences in the Uranian, that these bring those passions or those unruly conditions that may not be subdued by force, but conquered, guided and led in love. One that [when] guided aright may make same manifest in many ways, as meted in justice, and as given in literature. For these, as seen, to many, become the thought of this entity.

One that is mindful of conditions and doesn't desire to see anything or anyone suffer. While the idea of tease or taunt is seen at times, most is [a] direct debt toward those that would persecute another.

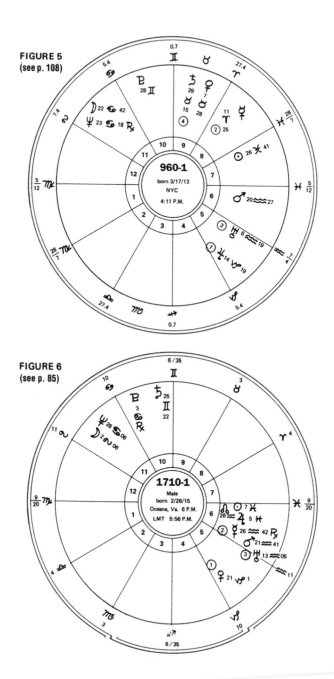

FIGURE 5
(see p. 108)

960-1
born 3/17/13
NYC
4:11 P.M.

FIGURE 6
(see p. 85)

1710-1
Male
born 2/26/15
Oceana, Va. 6 P.M.
LMT 5:56 P.M.

Appendix II

Zodiac—Planetary Signs and Symbols

For those readers unfamiliar with the symbols and terminology of traditional astrology, the following appendix and glossary are included. This material has been compiled from standard texts and references, along with explanations from the readings where noted.

TABLE A
SIGNS OF THE ZODIAC

ZODIAC HEMISPHERE (N-S)	SIGN SYMBOL	PROPHET DISCIPLE	RULING PLANET (Body Parts)	MASC. FEM.
I — Aries—(N) (Mar. 21-Apr. 20)	Ram (Fire)	Malachi Mathias (Mark)	Mars (Head & Face)	♂
II — Taurus—(N) (April 21-May 21)	Bull (Earth)	Haggai Thaddeus	Venus (Throat & Neck)	♀
III — Gemini—(N) (May 22-June 21)	Twins (Air)	Zachariah Simeon-Simon	Mercury (Hands, Shoulders, Lungs & Nerves)	♂
IV — Cancer—(N) (June 22-July 23)	Crab (Water)	Amos John	Moon (Breast & Stomach)	♀
V — Leo—(N) (July 24-Aug. 23)	Lion (Fire)	Michael-Hosea Jacob (James)	Sun (Heart, Sides, Upper Back)	♂
VI — Virgo—(N) (Aug. 24-Sept. 23)	Virgin (Earth)	Isaiah Thomas	Mercury (Solar Plexus, Bowels)	♀
VII — Libra—(S) (Sept. 24-Oct. 23)	Scale Bearer (Air)	Luke	Venus (Kidneys, Lower Back)	♂
VIII — Scorpio—(S) (Oct. 24-Nov. 22)	Scorpion (Water)	Judas	Pluto (Bladder, Sex Organs)	♀
IX — Sagittarius—(S) (Nov. 23-Dec. 21)	The Archer (Fire)	Zephaniah-St. George Andrew	Jupiter (Liver, Blood, Hips & Thighs)	♂
X — Capricorn—(S) (Dec. 22-Jan. 20)	Goat (Earth)	Jonah-Nahum Peter	Saturn (Knees & Spleen)	♀
XI — Aquarius—(S) (Jan. 21-Feb. 19)	Water Bearer (Air)	Matthew	Uranus (Ankles, Calves, Fluids—Intuition)	♂
XII — Pisces—(S) (Feb. 20-Mar. 20)	Fish (Water)	Joel James (Less)	Neptune (Feet—Psychic Faculty)	♀

TABLE B
PLANETARY SIGNS—PLANETARY DIGNITIES

PLANET	MASC. FEM.	SYMBOL	RULES (Strength)	GLAND*	HOUSE	DETRIMENT (Loss of Power)	EXALTATION (Harmony)	FALL
Sun	♂	Fire	Leo		5	Aquarius	Aries	Libra
Mercury		Fire	Gemini Virgo	Pineal	3 6	Sagittarius Pisces	Gemini	Sagittarius
Venus	♀	Water	Taurus Libra	Thymus	2 7	Scorpio Aries	Pisces	Virgo
Moon	♀	Water	Cancer		4	Capricorn	Taurus	Scorpio
Mars	♂	Fire	Aries	Adrenals	1	Libra Taurus	Capricorn	Cancer
Jupiter		Fire	Sagittarius Pisces	Pituitary	9 12	Gemini Virgo	Cancer	Capricorn
Saturn		Earth	Capricorn Aquarius	Gonads	10 11	Leo Cancer	Libra	Aries
Uranus		Air	Aquarius	Thyroid	11	Leo	Scorpio	Taurus
Neptune		Water	Pisces	Lyden	12	Virgo	Leo	Aquarius
Pluto	♂	Fire	Scorpio		8	Libra	Aquarius	Leo

*Glandular relationships are noted as from the readings.

TABLE C
HOUSES

I   **Personality**—Worldly Outlook.
Head and Face. Health, Childhood, Temperament.

II   **Finances**—Gain or Loss.
Throat and Ears. Liberty (Freedom)

III   **Brethren**—Mental Inclinations—Study—Writing—Short Journeys.
Shoulders, Hands, Arms—Lungs, Nervous System, Relatives.

IV   **Father**—Home, Environment—Lands, Property.
Breast, Stomach, Digestion.

V   **Children**—Love Affairs, Emotions, Speculation, Games, Theatre. Athletics and Sports. Physical/Mental Joys.
Heart, Sides, Upper Back.

VI   **Health**—Food, Hygiene, Clothing, Service (Work).
Solar Plexus, Bowels.

VII   **Personal Relationships**—Marriage, Partnerships, Contracts, Unions, Open Enemies, etc. (Partner's 1st House)
Kidneys, Ovaries, Veins, Lower Back.

VIII   **Death**—Legacies, Astral Flight, Sex.
Muscles, Bladder, Loins, Sex Organs.

IX   **Travel**—Education, Psychic Experiences, Philosophy, Religion.
Liver, Thighs.

X   **Mother**—Profession or Occupation, Country or Government.
Knees.

XI   **Friends**—Associations, Hopes and Wishes, Spiritual Joy. Clubs, Societies, Humanitarian Work.
Ankles.

XII   **Unseen or Unexpected Troubles**—Sorrows, Suffering, Secret Enemies. (Understanding) Charity, Sympathy, Hospitals, Penal Institutions.
Feet.

TABLE D
Houses—(Kinds)

Angular— (1 - 4 - 7 - 10) Planets in these houses have greater scope for dynamic action.

Succedent— (Fixed—2, 5, 8, 11) (After the Angular) Planets in these tend to stability, purpose, willpower.

Cadent— (3- 6- 9-12)
Adaptability, communication and ability to get along.

Houses of Life— (1 - 5 - 9)

Houses of Endings— (4 - 8 - 12)

Houses of Substance— (2 - 6 - 10)

Houses of Relationships— (3 - 7 - 11)

TABLE E
ZODIACAL SIGNS

TRIPLICITIES—

CARDINAL SIGNS—	ARIES	CANCER	LIBRA	CAPRICORN
(Restless as in Angular Houses)	(Mars) Self	(Moon)	(Venus) Mate	(Saturn) Position
FIXED SIGNS—	TAURUS	LEO	SCORPIO	AQUARIUS
(Resist change)	(Venus) Money	(Sun)	(Mars) Sex	(Saturn, Uranus) Wishes
MUTABLE/COMMON—	GEMINI	VIRGO	SAGITTARIUS	PISCES
(Adaptability)	(Mercury) Mind to Matter	(Mercury)	(Jupiter) Law-Religion	(Neptune) Cause-Effect

QUADRUPLICITIES—

FIRE	EARTH	AIR	WATER
Aries	Taurus	Gemini	Cancer
Leo	Virgo	Libra	Scorpio
Sagittarius	Capricorn	Aquarius	Pisces

Glossary*

AKASHA—Soul record.

ANGLES—See Aspects.

ASCENDANT—That sign of the zodiac (and degree) rising on the horizon at the moment of birth. (See Rising Sign.)

ASPECTS—Relationships, by angle or degree, of planets and zodiacal signs. Major aspects are those considered most influential in an individual chart or horoscope. These include: (±5°) Conjunctions—0°, Trines—120°, Sextiles—60°, Oppositions—180°, Squares—90°.

BIRTH CHART—Natal chart or horoscope.

CABALISTIC—(R) Pertaining to the Cabala. Based on mystical methods of interpreting Scripture and foretelling the future.

CONSTELLATIONS—Groups of stars seen in the heavens. Those which overlap the ecliptic (or great path of the Sun) are those termed of the zodiac; Aries, Taurus, Gemini, etc.

COSMIC INFLUENCES—(R) From the cosmos, or outer space; outside our own solar system.

CUSPS—That point or area where two signs of the zodiac (or two houses) merge.

CYCLES—(R) See chapter 6.

DEGREES—Signs of the zodiac are measured in degrees (longitude) along the ecliptic, 30° to each sign. Planetary positions (noon of every day) can be found in Raphael's Ephemeris for the year where the noon position in degrees is given for each day. **Sensitive degrees** in a chart are those occupied by a planet or cut by an angle (aspect) of the chart. Midpoints between planets are also significant.

---

*Terms interpreted from or generic to the readings are noted with an (R).

DESCENDANT—The point on the chart (or on the ecliptic) exactly opposite (180°) the ascendant.

DIMENSIONS—(R) A framework of mental relationships (or "vibrations"), eight in all—each represented by a planet. Example: Earth represents the third dimension.

ECLIPTIC—The great circle around which the Sun appears to travel in a year.

> **Plane of the Ecliptic**—The level on which the circle of the ecliptic lies, projected to infinity. (Planes in general are the extension in space of any of the Great Circles.)

ENTITY—(R) See Soul Entity.

ENVIRONS—(R) The readings use environs (accent on the "vi" syllable) almost exclusively to designate the soul's sojourns in planetary dimensions between earth lives, although sometimes the phrase "present environs" is used to mean present-life circumstances.

EQUINOX—"Equal night" at 0° Aries and 0° Libra. The beginning of spring and fall, or vernal/autumnal equinoxes.

ESOTERIC—(as in astrology) Hidden or secret. Known only by the select or few.

FIXED STARS—So called because they are so distant from Earth that they maintain their relative positions and form recognizable constellations or groups of stars. An entire group may appear to rise or set owing to the rotation of the Earth on its axis. The farther the group is from the ecliptic, the less it appears to move, until (Northern Hemisphere) the Pole Star (Polaris) remains as a fixed point and can be thought of as the hub of the Earth's orbit.

GEOCENTRIC—Considered as viewed from the Earth's center. Compare Heliocentric, as viewed from center of the Sun.

GREAT CIRCLE—Any circle, the plane of which passes through the center of the Earth.

HELIOCENTRIC—As viewed from the center of the Sun.

HOROSCOPE—The natal or birth chart and its relationship to the present incarnation.

HOUSES—Twelve in all. They number counterclockwise from the ascendant. (See appendix.)

I.C.—(Immum Coeli) Opposite the M.C. or midheaven, 90° below the ascendant on a natal chart.

INNATE—(Latent) See chapter 1.

KARMA—(Law of) Cause and effect. Or "As ye sow, so shall ye reap. As ye condemn, so are ye condemned. As ye forgive, so may ye be forgiven." (Galations 6:7; Luke 6:37)

LATENT—Undeveloped, hidden, or concealed.

MANIFESTED—A trait being developed or revealed.

MIDHEAVEN—(M.C.) The zenith, 90° above the ascendant on a natal chart. Opposite I.C.

MYSTIC—(R) Spiritually significant or symbolic as pertaining to spirit (not spiritualism) and the mysteries; a person believing in, or initiated into, the mysteries—By insight or immediate intuition in a state of spiritual ecstasy. (See Occult.)

NADIR—Opposite the zenith. (Not to be confused with I.C.)

NATAL CHART—Birth chart or horoscope.

OCCULT—(R) Mysterious; supernatural. Pertaining to the hidden sciences—magic, astrology, numerology, metaphysics, phenomenology, etc. (Not to be confused with mysticism. See Mystic and Spiritualism.)

PLANE—(R) A level of consciousness. There are said to be twelve in our solar system, symbolized by the zodiac. (See Ecliptic.)

PLANET—"Wanderer." A heavenly body which orbits around a central sun. (See Solar System.)

PROGRESSIONS As in a "progressed" chart. Requires further calculations based on the natal chart which enable the astrologer to study the trends over a given period of time.

PSYCHIC FORCES—(R) Pertaining to the psychic, or soul; mental, spiritual aspects. (Conscious, subconscious, superconscious aspects combined.)

RISING SIGN—Due to the Earth's rotation our Sun *appears* to rise on the horizon. On the first full day of spring, if we watch the sunrise, we shall be viewing that section of the zodiac known as Aries; a month later it will be Taurus, the next month Gemini, etc.

Two hours after sunrise (in Aries), Taurus will be rising; then Gemini two hours later, etc., until all twelve signs have risen above the horizon (each taking two hours) and we are greeted by another new day, again in Aries.

Therefore, twelve children, each born two hours apart on a single day, could have twelve different rising signs. (Along with twelve separate house arrangements governing the individual's planetary aspects.)

RULING PLANET—Each sign of the zodiac has a planet said to be its ruler or in affinity with it. (See appendix II, tables A and B.)

SEPTIMUS—(R) A planet referred to in the readings prior to 1930—Thought to be Pluto.

SIGNS—See Zodiac.

SOJOURNS—(R) The readings refer to "sojourns in the Earth," meaning the present and previous incarnations. They refer also to sojourns in planetary dimensions or planes of consciousness outside the Earth (between lives). The words *appearance* or *material* (sojourns) are generally used for incarnations in the Earth.

SOLAR SYSTEM

The Sun—Center of the solar system. Self-luminous. The other planets in the system shine in the reflected light of the Sun.

Diameter: 109 times that of Earth (864,000 miles).

Mass: 333,000 times that of Earth.

It rotates on its axis once every 25 days.

The Moon—A satellite of Earth. Its light, like that of the planets, is reflected from the Sun.

Diameter: 2,160 miles.

Revolution round Earth: 27 days, 7 hours, 43.2 minutes (sideral period).

Rotation: once in every revolution, so that the same face is nearly always presented to the Earth.

Mercury—Nearest planet to the Sun (36 million miles).

Diameter: 3,100 miles.

Mass: 1/27 that of Earth.

Revolution round Sun: 88 days.

Rotation: only once in its circling of the Sun so that it always (or nearly) presents the same face to the Sun, as the Moon does to the Earth.

Venus—67 million miles from Sun.

Slightly smaller than Earth.

Revolution round Sun: 225 days.

Rotation: 243 days.

Mars—141 million miles from Sun.

Diameter: half that of Earth (4,200 miles).

Mass: 1/9 that of Earth.

Revolution round Sun: 687 days.

Rotation period: 24 hours, 37 minutes.

It has two moons.

Jupiter—480 million miles from Sun.

Diameter: 88,000 miles.

Mass: 316 times that of Earth.

Revolution round Sun: almost 12 years.

Rotation: about 10 hours.

It has over seventeen satellites or moons, some as distant from it as 20,000 miles. Four of these revolve in the opposite direction to the rest.

Saturn—000 million miles from Sun.

Diameter: 71,000 miles.

Mass: 95 times that of Earth.

Revolution round Sun: 30 years.

Rotation: a little more than 10 hours.

Saturn has a series of rings composed of small particles. These lie in a plane inclined to the ecliptic at about 28°. There are ten moons outside the rings, one of which is very small and moving in an opposite direction to the rest. Since 1995 the total number of moons has come to at least twenty-four.

Uranus—1.8 billion miles from Sun.

Diameter: 32,000 miles.

Mass: 15 times that of Earth.

Revolution round Sun: 84 years.

Rotation: 16.8 hours.

Uranus was discovered in 1781 by the astronomer Herschel. It has five satellites, four of which revolve in a plane perpendicular to the ecliptic and in a retrograde direction.

Neptune—2.8 billion miles from Sun.

Diameter: 30,600 miles.

Mass: 17 times that of Earth.

Revolution round Sun: 164 years.

Rotation: 16.1 hours.

Neptune was discovered by Adams and Verrier in 1846. It has eight satellites, one of which moves in a retrograde direction.

Pluto—About 3.6 billion miles from Sun.

Diameter: about the same as Mars.

Revolution round Sun: 247.7 years.

Discovered in 1930.

SOLSTICE— (Latin: *sol* or *sun; sistere,* to make stand.)

> **Summer solstice**, approximately June 21, when Sun enters the sign of Cancer. Hence Tropic of Cancer, the demarcating line of the northernmost point on Earth where the Sun can be seen directly overhead. On or near December 22 is the **winter solstice**,

when the Sun is directly overhead on the line of the Tropic of Capricorn and on this date Sun enters Capricorn. At these dates the Sun is at its farthest point from the equator, or maximum declination, and we have the longest or shortest day of the year.

SOUL-ENTITY—(R) (Q) "Does the soul's entity change in reincarnation?"

(A) "The *entity?* The soul is the *entity!* The entity is the soul and the mind and the body of same, see? These only enter matter, or a new house, in incarnations." (1494-1)

SPHERES—(R) Combinations of planes and dimensions of consciousness.

SPIRITUALISM—The practice of communicating (or attempting to communicate) with spirits of the dead, usually through a medium.

TRANSITS—Present or projected interrelationships (or angles) of the planets as they relate to the natal chart. See chapter 6.

VIBRATIONS—(R) See p. 35.

ZENITH—The midheaven, directly overhead; 90° above ascendant, on a natal chart. Opposite nadir.

ZODIAC—(See appendix II.) A band of the heavens which extends 8° on either side of the Sun's apparent path (ecliptic). This circular band (360°) is divided into the twelve signs of the zodiac (30° each).

Beginning with 0° Aries they bear the same names as the constellations lying in the band of the zodiac with which they will coincide approximately every 26,000 years.

Part 2

The Music of the Spheres

Some Philosophical Notes on a New Age Astrology

> . . . become attuned, as it were, to the heavenly song, the heavenly music, the vibrations as it were of the spheres . . . 1487-1

I

Night. The music of nature swells around us in a vibrant chorus of insect calls and creature noises. Let us climb the hill to a higher promontory. Here an ocean of stars surrounds us, as far as the eye can see in every direction. And suddenly our little sphere, the Earth, is dwarfed by the utter magnitude of this outer sphere of limitless space, alive with the shimmering lights of distant constellations—"home" to how many millions of our brothers in the universe?

It has been estimated that there are a *hundred billion*

stars in our galaxy alone, all interconnected by an invisible network of nervelike pulsations and vibrations, forming the individual notes and collective harmonies that compose the wondrous music of the spheres. Mind-boggling? To be sure! Yet, consider:

The nearby Andromeda Galaxy is at least twice as large as our own Milky Way; and deep in space lie perhaps millions—nay, *billions*—of other galaxies, each with its unnumbered chorus of individual stars emitting their signal-like song . . .

The stars within a galaxy, like the cells in our own bodies, are born, reach maturity, and die, in an unending cycle of spirit merging into matter and moving out again.[1] Yet the galactic body itself retains its given shape, though its manifest substance is constantly fading and reforming. It assumes a pattern, moreover, that is unique in the heavens, distinguishable from all of its sister galaxies throughout the endless reaches of space, so that no two galaxies are quite alike, even as no two blades of grass on our little earth are ever identical. And do we not sense in this fact a profound significance? Do they not, these celestial cells called galaxies, comprise in their individual and collective essence a representation of the Body of God, even as does Man himself, and all of Nature? For all are One. All bear the imprimatur of Mind the Maker, from which they emanate, and of which they are part and parcel:

It should be understood that Life is One . . . 294-155

. . . ye are part and parcel of a universal consciousness, or God—and thus [part of] all that is within the universal consciousness, or the universal awareness; as the stars, the planets, the sun, the moon. 2794-3

Then, the Destiny of the Soul—as *of all creation*—
is to be one with Him; continually growing, growing, for that association. [Author's italics] 262-88

... the coming into the earth has been and is for
the evolution or the evolving of the soul unto its
awareness ... 5749-5

... in patience we become aware of our souls, of
our identity, of our being each a corpuscle, as it were,
in the great body, in the heart, of our God. 262-114

In amplification of these very profound concepts, the
Edgar Cayce readings make it clear that "each entity is
an universe within its own self ... " (279-15) We are told
that "the soul of man, thy soul, encompasses *all* in this
solar system or in others," (5755-2) and that "The *body* is
a pattern, it is an ensample of all the forces of the universe itself." (2153-6)

Such utterances have the freshness of revelation
about them. And quite rightly so! Yet, two great spiritual
figures of the past—Paracelsus and Swedenborg—had a
surprisingly similar vision of man and the universe.

"Heaven is man," wrote Paracelsus, in terms reminis-
cent of the cabbalistic Tree of Life, "and man is heaven,
and all men together are the one heaven, and heaven is
nothing but one man."[2] Then, in a logical sequel to that
esoteric statement, the great sixteenth-century physi-
cian-philosopher added another, which epitomizes the
whole of astrology: "Therefore the starry vault imprints
itself on the inner heaven of a man."[3]

A couple of centuries later, Emanuel Swedenborg, the
famous Swedish scientist who suddenly became a psychic, thus drastically altering the course of his career almost overnight, expressed essentially the same idea. But
he put it in novel terms that equate the material universe

with a stage or theatre, as it were, corresponding in an altered sense to the Heavenly Kingdom and the Lord Himself, where the incoming soul must act out its evolution under a human form, drawing its pattern from the very universe itself:

> The visible universe is nothing else than a theatre representative of the Lord's kingdom, and [this kingdom] is a theatre representative of the Lord Himself . . . And as he thus acts in unity with the angels, [a man] is also an image of heaven . . . under a human form.[4]

We find the Swedenborgian imagery closely paralleled in a number of further excerpts from the Edgar Cayce readings:

> . . . each soul that manifests itself in human form *is* thy brother—and the spirit and soul of same is in the form of thy Maker. 254-91

> And ye must be one—one with another, one with Him—if ye would be, as indeed ye are—corpuscles in the *life flow of* thy Redeemer! 1391-1

> Then those so entering *must* continue through the earth until the body-mind is made perfect for the soul, or the body-celestial again. 262-99

The Swedenborgian concept of a stage, or theatre, in relation to the soul's passage through the visible universe, is conveyed in the following excerpts:

> Though the conditions about you, about any soul, may be as torments . . . they are only used as puppets, and are as nothing . . . 256-5

In *Him* is the understanding, *by* and through those influences that have taken form—in universes—to meet the needs of each soul—that we might find our way to Him. 5755-2

For, without passing through each and every stage of development, there is not the correct vibration to become one with the Creator . . . 900-16

Though the earth, though the stars, may pass away; though there may be changes in the universe as to relative position, these are brought about by those combinations of that speck of human activity as relative *to* the soul's expression in any sphere of experience. 1297-1

" . . . [I]n passing through the law," the readings tell us, "we may become perfect, but not in materiality." (5252-1)

Man's development, as given, is of man's understanding and applying the laws of the Universe, and as man applies those, man develops, man brings up the whole generation of man. 900-70

. . . for man was created a little bit higher than all the rest of the whole universe, and is capable of harnessing, directing, enforcing the laws of the universe. 5-2

The first laws, then, partook of that of the study of self, the division of mind, the division of the solar systems, the division of man in the various spheres of existence through the earth plane and through the earth's solar system. 5748-2

" . . . [F]lesh," according to the readings, " . . . is the testing portion of the universal vibration." (900-16) For this reason, many earthly cycles may be necessary, as well as repeated sojourns elsewhere in the solar system between incarnations. "For, those sojourns are as lessons, as grades . . . " (3226-1) But with the application of the lessons learned, and the gradual mastery of the universal laws, an advanced soul-entity is ready to move on through "those centers about which thine own solar system moves—in Arcturus," (5755-1) to experience higher and higher "dimension[s] of consciousness or awareness" (5755-2):

> When an individual incarnates in the earth, he has *possibly* passed through all the various spheres, either once, twice, *many* times . . . 311-2

> Not as a physical body as known in the earth, but as a body adaptable to the environs of [for example] Jupiter; for there's life there (not as known in earth), as there is in Saturn, Sun, Moon, Venus, Mercury, Uranus, Neptune, Mars [and Pluto[5]]; all have their form . . . The elements about same are inhabited, if you choose, by those of their own peculiar environment. 630-2

> . . . as long as an entity is within the confines of that termed the earth's and the sons of the earth's solar system, the developments are within the sojourns of the entity from sphere to sphere; and when completed it begins—throughout the music of the spheres with Arcturus, Polaris, and through those sojourns in the outer sphere. 441-1

> For man is not made for this world alone. 4082-1

... all [worlds] are the work of His hand, are thine to possess, thine to use—as one with Him. 5755-2

"In my Father's house are many mansions," Jesus told His disciples. We may regard His words as a reference to the soul's habitations as it moves through those countless spheres of evolving awareness or consciousness that constitute our experience in the visible universe, each stage corresponding, as it were, to a different and higher rate of vibration. Yet, in a more spiritual sense, Jesus was undoubtedly alluding to a place in the Heavenly Kingdom—the "New Jerusalem"—where the purged and purified soul regains the body-celestial, at last, in that perfect union with its Source—the Universal Consciousness, or God:

In that city, in that place, there is no need of the sun, nor of the moon, nor the stars; for He is the *Light;* He *is* Light, and in Him is no darkness at all! 262-115

Spiritually there becomes no time or space, for they—like the Father—are one. 2879-1

Do not think it is a different universe. No. It is the same universe you see about you, even now, though dimly perceived and little understood at present. What is changed, then? It is the soul's awareness of its Self.

II

To reach a "New Age" understanding of astrological principles, we must begin from a spiritual premise. What better premise than the Word Itself?

Then in considering those conditions, those ex-

periences as may be a part of the soul's awareness—
in the beginning was the Word, and the Word was
God, and the Word was with God. *That* is the
premise. 5755-2

And the Word became flesh.

In the Edgar Cayce readings, we find this stunning
summary of the development of that Soul-entity who
first came into the earth plane in "thought form" as
Amilius, took on fleshly woes as Adam, and went through
some thirty incarnations before completing His own development through our solar system as Jesus, the risen
Christ, who became One with the Father, and the Pattern for all of us who choose to follow:

> In the Creation, we find all force relative one with
> the other, and in the earth's plane that of the flesh.
> In the developing from plane to plane becomes the
> ramification, or the condition of the will merited in
> its existence finding itself through eons of time.
>
> In the illustration, or manifestation in this, we
> find again in the man called Jesus.
>
> When the soul reached that development in
> which it reached earth's plane, it became in the flesh
> the model, as it had reached through the develop-
> ments in those spheres, or planets, known in the
> earth's plane, obtaining then One in All.
>
> As in Mercury pertaining of Mind.
>
> In Mars of Madness.
>
> In Earth as of Flesh.
>
> In Venus as Love.
>
> In Jupiter as Strength.
>
> In Saturn as the beginning of earthly woes, that
> to which all insufficient matter is cast for the begin-
> ning [over again].
>
> In that of Uranus as of the Psychic.

In that of Neptune as of Mystic.

In Septimus [Pluto?] as of [Cosmic?] Consciousness.

In Arcturus as of the developing . . .

In this man called Jesus we find at a One-ness with the Father, the Creator, passing through all the various stages of development. In mental perfect, in wrath perfect, in flesh made perfect, in love become perfect, in death become perfect, in psychic become perfect, in mystic become perfect, in consciousness become perfect, in the greater ruling forces [represented in Arcturus] *becoming* perfect, and is as the model, and through the compliance with such laws made perfect, destiny, the pre-destined, the fore-thought, the will, made perfect, the condition made perfect, is an ensample for man, and only as a man, for He lived only as man. He died as man. [Author's italics] 900-10

The influences ascribed to the various planets, in functioning as developmental forces for the evolving Christ—He who became "the Way"—coincide very closely with the teachings of orthodox astrology (although the reference to Arcturus certainly introduces an unfamiliar dimension, both literally and figuratively!). As "schooling centers" for the soul, so to speak, each of the planets may wield a positive or negative influence on our soul development in the earth as we come under its particular vibration, depending upon a host of factors. Environment and heredity are most often cited. Esoterically considered, however, these reflect the soul's choice, based on what each entity has built for itself through its various earthly and planetary sojourns. We are not the victims of fate, but creatures of our own designing. And free will is ever paramount in our choices and decisions. Thus, when passing under the influence of any planetary aspect, for weal or woe, everything depends upon our freely determined reactions. Opportunities may be converted into pitfalls, and vice versa.

Here is a brief summary of the influences associated with each of the planets.

Mercury pertains to mental development. In the readings, a great number of corroborative references occur, such as this one: "In Mercury [we find] the high mental abilities . . . " (1981-1) From an astrological standpoint, this would appear to suggest that Mercury may have been rising, or at a midheaven position, at the moment of [1981]'s birth, since either of these two configurations in a natal chart indicates a particularly influential role for the planet—or planets—involved, as we shall see later. Or Mercury may have been "favorably aspected" in some other manner in the individual's horoscope, thus aiding its beneficial influence; even as the reverse may be true of any sign or planet in a birth chart, reflecting what an incoming entity has meted for itself, to aid its own spiritual growth and development in a given incarnation. The negative traits of Mercury, of course, are seen in that tendency to abuse one's mental gifts to the detriment of self and others; and this could lead to an "unfavorably aspected" Mercury in one's next earthly cycle, with the mental powers afflicted in some manner.

Venus symbolizes love, art, and beauty, which may turn to the extremes of lust and decadence in their more material or negative phases. The spiritual aspects of Venus are evident in the following excerpt from reading 5755-1—but with a qualification added, which suggests the negative traits also: "What is love? Then what is Venus? It is beauty, love, hope, charity—yet all of these have their extremes."

Mars is referred to in astrology as the Energizer, and its characteristics are action and courage, while its negative connotations would be uncontrolled rage and anger. "In Mars of Madness," says reading 900-10. But in another reading, a more positive view is given: "From Mars we find the urges for activity, the intenseness with which the entity gives itself to that it chooses." (3299-1) *Jupiter* represents the ennobling forces, according to both astrology and the readings. Magnanimity and benevolence are Jupiterian traits. "In Jupiter we find abilities in a helpful, universal way and manner," says reading 3299-1. Carried to its negative extreme, however, extravagance and self-indulgence are manifested, as the readings testify.

Saturn is called the Taskmaster; its traditional role in astrology is to promote patience and endurance under stress. The readings call it the planet of "sudden or violent changes . . . And yet these are testing periods of thy endurance, of thy patience, of thy love of truth, harmony and the spirit that faileth not." (1981-1)

Uranus, in the terms of orthodox astrology, is equated with the Psychic. This conforms with the interpretation in the readings. In its negative aspect, however, Uranus is associated with eccentricity and the extremes: "From the Uranian influences we find the extremist." (1206-3)

Neptune is the Mystic. It is also associated with water, as might be expected of one who explores the mysterious depths of the universe. Its negative connotations are those tendencies to overdo a love of mystery and the occult forces. "One that should have been guided close in the study of those things pertaining to the mystery and the occult," says reading 2213-1, relevant to the Neptunian influences.

Pluto, which was not discovered by modern astronomers until 1930, is believed to have been the planet sometimes referred to in the Edgar Cayce readings as Septimus or Vulcan (in fact, reading 826-8 confirms the synonymity with Vulcan); and this suggests that the most distant planet in our solar system may once have been known to the ancients—intuitively or otherwise—and was identified by them under different names than now. Modern astrology has little to say concerning this relatively unknown planet, although it is credited as a broadly "regenerative" influence on mankind in its positive aspect, and a calamitous one in its negative forces. This appears to be an accurate assessment, if we may judge by the following excerpts from the readings: "It [Pluto's influence] is gradually *growing,* and thus is one of those influences that are to be as a demonstrative activity in the future affairs or developments of man towards the spiritual-minded influences, or those influences outside of himself." (1100-27) On the negative side, reading 1735-2 contains a cautionary note to "beware of fire, and especially of firearms, or explosives," referring to "the influences that bring for warnings, as seen in Mars and Vulcan [Pluto] . . . "

Seven of the planets have a relative correspondence with the seven endocrine glands, as presented in reading 281-29. These glands are viewed in the readings as a conjoined system, or "chain," of physical centers directly linked to our *psychic* evolution. (In esoteric literature, it is stated that each of the endocrine centers has its counterpart in the etheric body, and these are called *chakras.)* Here, then, are the given planetary correspondences: Mercury, the pineal gland; Venus, the thymus; Mars, the solar plexus; Jupiter, the pituitary gland; Saturn, the gonads; Uranus, the thyroid; Neptune, the lyden gland. Pluto, as a gradually growing influence, may not be directly associated in any way with the endocrine system itself, although the nature of its evolving influence implies an indirect connection of some kind with the higher centers. (Some might envision a correlation with the "beam of light" associated with the "crown chakra," in mystical literature.)

The individual vibration of each of the various planetary bodies is also expressed in color, as well as sound. For, "music, color, vibration are all a part of the planets, just as the planets are a part—and a pattern—of the whole universe." (5755-1) (The notes and colors of some of the planets are detailed in an essay written by Edgar Cayce, with Thomas Sugrue, and published by the A.R.E. Press under the title, *Auras.*)

And what of that governing luminary of our solar system, the Sun? Esoteric astrology, following the spiritual tradition of the medieval alchemists, assigns a mystical unity between the Sun and "the Son," or the Christ. Elsewhere in the symbolism of alchemy, Sun and Moon are representational of Adam and Eve, and they embody the male/female, yang/yin principles. The Sun is associated with the heart, and its nature is fire; while the Moon typifies the imaginative forces and intuition, and its nature is water.

Sun and Moon play dominant roles in our earthly lives, of course, and are obviously important in astrology. In fact, the evolving soul-entity may even have experienced indwellings in their environs at one time, between earthly cycles:

> . . . the being translated in materiality as Ra Ta— was from the infinity forces, or from the Sun . . .
> 5755-1

> . . . the dwellers upon the Moon (the satellite of the earth) preceded the abilities for matter . . . And this entity was among those that so dwelt, and is influenced by two sojourns there. 264-31

In astrology, the Sun is a "positive" force. Its position in the natal chart, and its governing sign, form a general guide to the basic character of the individual. The Moon, as a passive or "negative" body, whose subtle influence on the tides can also exert a pull on our bodily fluids, as well as altering our moods and feelings, is indicative of the intuitional and emotional forces affecting the soul-entity throughout its earthly sojourns. The nature of its influence depends, as with the Sun and all of the various planets and signs in a horoscope, upon its location and aspects within the twelve divisions or "houses" of the horoscope, as well as upon the individual's exercise of its divine right of free will and choice:

There is set before thee two ways, ever . . . 347-2

. . . the soul must make its choice; as to whether things are to be viewed from the material angle or from the soul's development—that must live on and on . . . For, will and choice is the gift of the soul . . . 556-1

. . . the will of a soul, of a body, is supreme . . . 416-2

As to the application of self respecting the astrological forces—these . . . are only urges. As to what one does *with* and about same depends upon choices made. 1710-3

Yet the influence of astrological forces cannot be ignored with impunity, since these forces operate within the framework of universal law, representing distinct dimensions of consciousness or awareness that each soul must meet:

. . . there is the influence of the planets upon an individual, for all must come under such influence . . . 3744-4

Hence the sun, the moon, the stars, the position in the heavens or in all of the hosts of the solar systems that the earth occupies—all have their influence . . . 5753-1

Each planetary influence vibrates at a different rate of vibration. An entity entering that influence enters that vibration . . . 281-55

. . . it is not so much that an entity is influenced because the Moon is in Aquarius or the Sun in Capricorn or Venus or Mercury in that or the other house, sign, or the Moon and Sun sign, in that one of the planets is in this or that position in the heavens; but rather because those positions in the heaven are from the *entity* having been in that sojourn as a soul! This is how the planets have the greater influence in the earth upon the entity, see? 630-2

Earth, in this solar system, merely represents three dimensions. Then how many dimensions are in this solar system? Eight! What position does the earth occupy? Third! What position do others occupy? That relative relationship one to another. 5755-2

. . . but there may be as seven [dimensions], in Mercury—or four, in Venus—or five, as in Jupiter. There may be only one as in Mars. There may be many more as in those of Neptune, or they may become even as nil—until purified in Saturn's fires. 311-2

Intriguing indeed is the probability that our space probes into the solar system, bringing back to us glimpses of Uranus and Jupiter and other planetary bodies in the limited terms of our three-dimensional vision, have brought us no closer to the "reality" of these planets than looking at a locked jewel-box can reveal to our eyes the multifaceted beauty of the gems inside . . . Moving in the psychic realm, however, it is conceivable that one might "shift dimensions," as it were, by raising or lowering the vibratory rate, and thus gain entrance into the reality of these other worlds. In fact, it is primarily at this *psychic* level, apparently, that planetary influences are felt upon our lives in the earth plane.[6]

To an entity in the earth plane, as Cayce explained it, astrological influences arise as "mental urges" only, while one's prior appearances in the earth create "the urges from the emotions" that have been built as influential forces. (633-2) As the readings make clear, there is an exquisite rationale underlying the concept of free will and choice in relation to the urges experienced; and the implications are indeed sobering:

> (Q) Comment upon the following. Is it worthy of expansion; that is, does it carry any light of truth?
> The Creator, in seeking to find or create a being worthy of companionship, realized that such a being would result only from a free will exercising its divine inheritance and through its own efforts find its Maker. Thus, to make the choice really a Divine one caused the existence of states of consciousness, that would indeed tax the free will of a soul; thus light and darkness. Truly, only those tried so as by fire can enter in.
> (A) The only variation that we would make is that all souls in the beginning were one with the Father. The separation, or turning away, brought evil. Then there became the necessity of the awareness of self's being out of accord with, or out of the realm of

blessedness; and, as given of the Son, "yet learned he obedience through the things which he suffered." 262-56

What is meted must be met. 442-3

For, each soul enters [the earth] that it may make its paths straight. 2021-1

Hence, Destiny is: "As ye sow, so shall ye reap." And like begets like! 276-7

The soul is complete only in the law and realm of its Creator. 553-1

III

The astrological influence most noticeably felt by a soul-entity in the earth is its vibratory attunement with the Sun.

This influence bears a corresponding relationship to the Sun's passage through one of the twelve zodiacal constellations at the time of the entity's birth. And we know these zodiacal correspondences, of course, as the twelve familiar Sun signs of traditional astrology. They represent those mythical figures, from the ram in Aries through the two fishes in Pisces, that lie along the path of our Sun in its annual orbit through the heavens.

However, due to the spinning motion of the earth, the twelve signs are encountered once again, in a much faster cycle, so that a different sign of the zodiac appears on the horizon every two hours within a twenty-four-hour period of the earth's daily rotation; and this introduces yet another phase of zodiacal influence on the entity, as we shall shortly explain.

Additionally, there is a much, much slower, "backward" passage through the twelve constellations of the zodiac as the slow wobbling of the earth causes its rotating axis to point to different parts of the sky at different times. This cycle takes almost 26,000 years to complete, and each transit through one of the twelve constellations is called an "Age." It lasts about 2,160 years. We are now moving out of the Piscean Age, as almost everyone knows, and into the Aquarian Age. Each 2,160-year cycle wields a general influence upon the whole body of mankind.

Now, to explain a bit . . .

A soul-entity born into the earth, say, when the Sun is transiting the constellation of Aries (from March 21 to April 19) will come under the direct influence of that particular Sun sign. This "timing" has actually been chosen by the incoming soul, in all likelihood, as the most suitable solar configuration for its current phase of development.[7] And it may have entered as an "Aries" in more than one of its former lives, repeating the soul's patient journey through the twelve different signs or expressions. For example:

> Coming under the influence of Pisces, or that making for a spiritual attunement, we find this— with the sojourns of the entity—is a portion of the entity's whole being.
>
> For *more than once* has the entity in its sojourns in the earth come under the influence of this same astrological aspect. [Author's italics] 1007-1

Yet each cycle will be on a higher rung of the ladder, so to speak, as the soul-entity makes its rounds—*unless, of course, it is slipping!*

If a soul-entity enters on the cusp between two Sun signs, so that its birth date is at the "tail-end" of the one sign's influence and the commencement of the other's, the attributes of *both* signs will likely be revealed or expressed in the individual's basic character; but the incoming sign will normally wield the preponderant influence.

Yet, there are other zodiacal influences, too, that come into special focus. Depending upon the hour of birth, and quite regardless of the particular Sun sign in a natal chart, we will find Scorpio, Taurus, or one of the other twelve figures of the zodiac rising on the horizon, as viewed from the perspective of the earth's daily rotation; and this will be known as the "ascendant sign" for that entity. Its influence may be felt and recognized as an aspect of the "revealed personality" in varying degree, depending in part upon which planets, if any, may be rising under the same sign to add their influence to the ascendant's innate force or influence. Additionally, the readings appear to suggest that the zodiacal sign and planetary bodies found in a horoscope at the "midheaven" position (more commonly termed the zenith) are also strongly influential. And this is in accord with traditional astrology, as well.

To ascertain the positions of the ascendant and zenith in a natal chart, simply visualize a circle divided into a quaternary by two dissecting lines in the form of a cross. The horizontal line, quite logically, represents the horizon. Its left-hand extremity marks the ascendant point, or moment of sunrise, while the right-hand extremity of the line marks the setting position, called the descendant. The vertical arm of the cross terminates at an upper point marking the zenith, or mid-day, while its lower extremity—called the nadir—represents midnight. Each quadrant of the circle is divided into three sections, or houses, constituting essentially thirty degrees of arc apiece, and running in a counterclockwise manner from the first house, just below the ascendant, to the twelfth, in a position just above the ascendant. Thus, if one is born at midnight, the Sun will be centered at the nadir, or base of the horoscope, on the cusp between the third and fourth houses. And if, additionally, one is an Arien (Aries), the cusp will bear the zodiacal sign of the ram at whatever "degree" applies in relation to the date and hour, based on the Sun's thirty-day transit (approximately) through that constellation.

Not too complicated, really. Any good astrological textbook will serve to familiarize the interested layman with the rudimentals of this fascinating subject. But let us continue.

First, here are the aforementioned excerpts from the readings that suggest the importance of both the natal Sun sign and the ascendant in a horoscope, as well as the zenith, and those planets rising or at midheaven at the moment of birth:

> The strongest force used in the destiny of man is the Sun first, then the closer planets to the earth, or those that are coming to *ascension* at the time of the birth of the individual . . . [Author's italics] 3744-4

> (Q) Are the tendencies of an individual influenced most by the planets nearer the earth at the time of the individual's birth?
> (A) At, or from that one which is at the *zenith* when the individual is in its place or sphere, or as is seen from that sphere or plane [from which] the soul and spirit took its flight in coming to the earth plane. [Author's italics] 3744-4

Most interestingly, Edgar Cayce's natal chart appears to confirm the nearly equal importance of both positions; for he had Uranus ("the Psychic") rising, while Neptune ("the Mystic") was in the ninth house, following the midheaven position, or what is termed the zenith in astrology, although Uranus's is the dominant influence. For, as stated in reading 5755-1, "From an astrological aspect, then, the greater influence at the entrance of this entity that ye call Cayce was from Uranus."

But going back to the two excerpts just cited from reading 3744-4, a contradiction of sorts is apparent, perhaps due to some obscurity in the wording. It raises a question as to whether it is the ascendant or the zenith in a horoscope that should actually be regarded as the more dominant planetary position or sign, normally speaking. (In astrology, the ascendant is typically regarded as the point of greater influence than the zenith, although both positions are "key" ones. Yet it depends, of course, upon the given configuration of the planets in a horoscope, which may have a modifying effect.)

A solution looms. It is quite conceivable that the sleeping Cayce, when he used the word "zenith," was actually referring (in quite proper, though uncommon, usage!) to the *horizon,* or point of ascension. For although the more common meaning of "zenith" is a vertical or midheaven position, we do find a secondary definition of zenith as *"the point of the horizon at which a heavenly body rises."* (!) This is confirmed in *The Complete Edition of the Oxford English Dictionary.* (In fact, reading 254-2 states that Edgar Cayce was born with "Uranus at its zenith," thus corroborating this interpretation. See on the following page Cayce's natal chart, with Uranus actually at *ascendant.)*

To those who remain unconvinced by this explanation, however, all uncertainty can perhaps be resolved by way of an unlikely source.

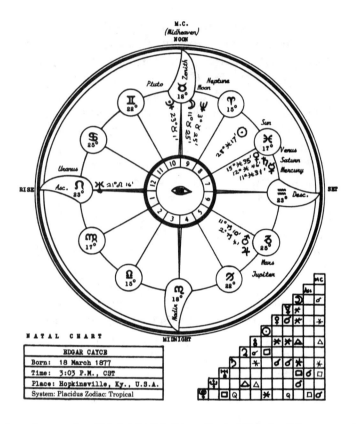

NATAL CHART

EDGAR CAYCE
Born: 18 March 1877
Time: 3:03 P.M., CST
Place: Hopkinsville, Ky., U.S.A.
System: Placidus Zodiac: Tropical

Based on reading 254-2, 3/19/19. (*Note:* Central Standard Time was not in existence in 1877, although it was being used in 1919, of course, when the reading was given. We have applied CST. However, there remains a question as to whether the reading may have referred, instead, to either Local Mean Time—which would have placed the ascendant at 21° 30' Leo—or Sun Time, with Leo at 22° on the ascendant.)

A noted French researcher and statistician, Michel Gauquelin, has conducted a detailed scientific study of cosmic rhythms in relation to the career groupings of some 25,000 successful Europeans.[8] We have previously challenged certain of his statistical conclusions[9] because his career categories were not sufficiently specialized to reveal meaningful statistics in respect to natal Sun signs, whose influence his rather broadly based statistical studies refuted. Yet a more specialized approach on our part in a convincing number of career classes yielded consistently positive results. Despite this friendly difference in our respective findings on Sun signs, however, it is worth noting that the frequency distribution of several of the planets observed by Gauquelin (Mars, Jupiter, Saturn, and the Moon) in relation to certain of his more generalized career categories—namely, champions, actors, scientists, and writers—did indeed manage to yield positive statistical results, despite the lack of specialization. Under a more specialized approach—such as "top achievers" among, say, boxers, comedians, astronomers, and novelists, as one set of possible choices in the four fields covered—we believe Gauquelin's findings might have proven even more significant for the four "positive" planets in his survey, as well as yielding similarly positive results for the remaining planets and the Sun, which lost any statistical significance in his too broadly based groupings. But it is not our intention to sound critical, for Gauquelin is an outstandingly fine and innovative researcher, and one who is continuing to contribute much to a more scientific understanding of astrological principles within a statistical format.

Our purpose here is to examine the results of his findings in respect to the four planets mentioned—namely, Mars, Jupiter, Saturn, and the Moon (the latter is loosely termed a "planet," in astrology). And those results would appear to indicate a statistical pattern applicable in varying degree to *any* of the planets, we maintain, if observed under a sufficiently specialized approach for career categories likely to be suitable for each planet, such as Uranus for famous psychics, Neptune for well-known mystics, and so on. (In addition to Cayce, by the way, Nostradamus was another famous psychic who had Uranus rising. This points in the direction of our theory, but would require a sufficiently large survey of well-known psychics to be statistically meaningful, of course.)

Gauquelin, in his statistical study of the natal horoscopes of "high achievers" in four different career categories, found Mars, Jupiter, Saturn, or the Moon, respectively, cresting in the area of the ascendant, first, and then the zenith, followed in sequential significance by the descendant and the nadir, although in markedly reduced prominence as compared to the former two areas.

There emerged one curious fact which merits emphasis: The actual "peak" of the four cresting curves occurred at a point "over the line," in each case, falling in what are termed the four cadent houses of a horoscope—namely, the twelfth, ninth, sixth, and third, in that order of importance. This contradicts orthodox astrology, which has always taught that the house on the "approaching" side of the quadrant marker (first, tenth, seventh, and fourth, respectively) is the more significant. So, based on the implications of Gauquelin's positive statistical results with at least four of the planets, the commonly accepted view about the relative unimportance of the cadent houses is certainly open to question. It will be the role of a "New Age" astrology to explore the implications of such a finding.

We come, now, to two areas of conflicting opinion in the modern practice of astrology.

One relates to whether the sidereal system of astrology, which is heliocentric or "Sun-oriented" in its approach to the casting of a natal horoscope, is more accurate than the earth-oriented geocentric system (called the "tropical") that is in common usage today in the West. Both systems have their ardent adherents, and certain technical justifications can be presented on behalf of each. We formerly leaned toward the sidereal, subject to some modifications in the Western practice of this system at the present time. But we have come across a reading[10] that appears to resolve the dispute in favor of the geocentric system:

> (Q) What is the correct system to use in astrology—the heliocentric or the geocentric system?
> (A) . . . the Persian—or the geocentric—is the nearer correct. 933-3

This does not leave totally unresolved a number of other perplexing questions of a related nature; but we are confident that the astrologers will ultimately find the answers for themselves as they continue to seek for them.

The second area of debate is whether a natal chart should be based on the time of conception or the moment of birth; most astrologers would agree to the latter, and so do we. But if the latter, should the birth of the body-physical or the soul-body be the decisive factor? Here is what the readings say:

> (Q) Should an astrological horoscope be based on the time of physical birth or the time of soul birth?
> (A) On time of physical birth; for these are merely *inclinations,* and because of inclinations are not the influence of will. 826-8

> Hence the position or the period of the entrance [birth] is not *ruled* by the position [of Sun and planets] but it may *be judged* by the position as to the influence . . . [Author's italics] 1347-1

IV

From the beginning of time, man has sought to read the message of the stars. He has stood between heaven and earth, and has tried to discern in the face of the sky the path for his feet to follow. It has been a natural inclination on his part to gaze upward for guidance: his half-forgotten origins, after all, were celestial. The predictable outcome of all man's astral ponderings was the creation of a "divining art" which he called astrology. Down through the ages, that "art" has been "reworked" and redefined. Today it is viewed as an emergent science. Unlike astronomy, however, which is only concerned with looking outward for the answers, astrology also looks within. It seeks to decipher the celestial hieroglyphics by tracing the patterns of their influence upon human destiny. The problem, until recently, lay in the absence of a heavenly "Rosetta stone" to aid in deciphering a celestial language that abounds in symbols whose meanings are often interior and concealed. The result has been a veil of mystery and confusion that still lies between man and the stars.

We make bold to suggest that an astrological "Rosetta stone" now exists, although largely ignored and unrecognized. We refer to the voluminous body of the Edgar Cayce readings, with their countless references and insights on the subject of astrology, providing innumerable keys to its interpretation. Indeed, within the readings lie the roots for a whole new approach to the inner self, which might aptly be termed "Akashic Astrology."

Drawing on what are called the akashic records, which constitute that "Book of Life" written on the skein of time and space by each soul-entity throughout its total experience from the dawn of time, Edgar Cayce gave some 2,000 "life" readings, as they were termed. In these readings, he included astrological reference points and explanations pertaining to the more influential mental urges brought to bear on the individual in the present as a result of astrological sojourns elsewhere in the solar system between the entity's prior incarnation (or incarnations) in the earth and the present one, as modified by the individual's collective soul development or retrogression during earlier appearances in the earth. (Those previous lives having a direct impact on the present development were given.)

It is obvious that this sort of detailed information on literally hundreds of individuals, whose date and location of birth, sex, and occupation are also included in the transcript of each reading, must necessarily provide the astrological researcher with a highly promising reservoir of material from which a great number of meaningful statistical conclusions may be drawn. (Initial work in this direction, in fact, has already commenced on a limited basis, the preliminary findings, particularly as they relate to planetary aspects, are profoundly interesting.)

The eventual results, as more and more astrological researchers probe the wealth of data in the readings—including, in addition to the "life" readings, special readings touching on such related topics as the use of astrology in vocational guidance (5753-3), or heredity and environment (900-19, 900-23)—are apt to be surprising.

It will not be an easy task to organize and analyze the psychic information on astrology in the readings, but if pursued with patience and persistence it will enable the perceptive researcher to interpret many esoteric aspects of the subject that have heretofore defied a proper understanding. The results will revolutionize astrology as it exists today, setting it on a totally new and more spiritual foundation.

V

The twelve familiar figures of the zodiac have often

had other faces, other names. Not always have they been the ones we know today. Leo the Lion, for example, has been a dog, a cat, and an elephant in its gradual evolution from its Babylonian and Egyptian origins. In Chinese and Hindu astrological lore, moreover, the zodiacal asterisms bear utterly different animal representations than those that are popular in the West. Yet, the Edgar Cayce readings seem to subscribe to the view (although it is not anywhere stated in specific terms, to our knowledge) that certain psychological factors may play a determining role in setting the "right" symbols for us in any given phase of our development in a relative world, a relative universe. Thus, while once pointing out that our present placement of the Sun signs is "some two signs off," today (5755-1), other readings nevertheless did not hesitate to support the current symbolism now in use under the popular geocentric system of astrology. For example, an individual born with the Sun at 26° 58' Pisces, near the cusp of Aries, was told: " . . . coming near the cusps and under the influence of Pisces . . . " (282-2) In summary, it seems as if mankind, through its own mass beliefs, forming the "Collective Unconscious," is capable of influencing and even reshaping certain of the "stage props"—at least, here in the earth plane! For, "thoughts are things," as the readings repeatedly stress; and mind is indeed the builder of its own little universe, as well as contributing towards the "collective image" of the outer universe—the Macrocosm.

The influence of the signs, or cycles, of the zodiac is clearly confirmed in the readings:

> For various individuals, under various cycles, of course, are subject to changes as they pass through the various periods of the Zodiac. 3688-1

The study of the meaning of Aries, Sagittarius,

> Pisces, Libra, or any or all of such phases, would in-
> dicate the activity of the individual. For, remember,
> it is body manifestation . . . 5746-1

According to the readings, twelve is a number relating
to "the mystic forces," and is emblematic of "a *finished*
product, as is given in all forces in nature," and in those
"twelve combined forces" that brought into the world
"those strengths . . . as [were] necessary for a replenish-
ing of same." (5751-1) The twelve signs of the zodiac fit
into this category, of course, as do the twelve months of
the year, or the twelve tribes of Israel; and we are also
reminded of the twelve apostles.

St. Bede the Venerable, an English monk of the eighth
century, who was well known for his scholarly commentaries on the Bible, envisioned a mystical correspondence between the twelve apostles and the twelve signs
of the zodiac, which he set down in Latin for posterity,
although posterity has largely ignored his efforts. But
one of the readings, without any reference to the Venerable Bede, of whom Mr. Cayce had almost surely never
heard, confirmed the ancient monk's spiritual insight:

> As each of the twelve apostles represented major
> centers or regions or realms [constellations] through
> which consciousness became aware in the body of
> the earth itself, so did He find—as in thine own self
> ye find—those twelve stumbling stones . . . These
> are the price of flesh, of material consciousness,
> and are only passing. 2823-1

More recently, the well-known psychic, Jeane Dixon,
reportedly experienced a beautiful illumination while
kneeling in meditation at St. Matthew's Cathedral, in
Washington, D.C., followed by a more complete vision at
the same spot some few weeks later, in which she saw a

circle divided into twelve segments. Each segment contained the figure of an apostle and one of the twelve signs of the zodiac. The correlations, which form the basis of her book, *Yesterday, Today, and Forever*,[11] are shown in the chart on the following page. To these we have added our own interpretation—based on astrological teachings, in general, and corroborative data in the readings— of the "twelve stumbling stones" referred to by Edgar Cayce, under the heading, "Negative Trait"; while the column headed "Positive Trait" contains the opposite quality, by means of which each of the twelve stumbling stones to which we are *all* subject, at one phase or another of our earthly development, may be converted into a stepping-stone.

We conclude our comments in this regard with an interesting excerpt from the readings:

> ... all entities realize they in themselves are both positive and negative influences, and that the First Cause—or the Spirit—must of necessity within itself be likewise, yet more positive than negative, for it attracts with attraction and repels with rebellion of that same activity of which every entity is a part. 264-31

VI

As we move into the cusp of the Aquarian Age, with its many implications of spiritual change and promise, we may well pay heed to a highly curious astrological note

---

*According to reading 587-6, Jesus was actually born "on the 19th day of what could now be termed March." The symbolic significance of "the sign of the fish" in relation to the birth of Jesus, at the opening of the Piscean Age, is obvious. And although the apostles appointed a successor to Judas, in a real sense it was the resurrected Christ Himself who filled the twelfth seat, thus completing the circle, or cycle of signs, as Master of them all.

SIGN	APOSTLE	NEGATIVE TRAIT	POSITIVE TRAIT
Aries	Peter	Impulsiveness	Patience; Self-restraint
Taurus	Simon	Obstinacy	Flexibility; Adaptability
Gemini	James (the Less)	Doublemindedness	Singleness of Purpose
Cancer	Andrew	Hypersensitivity	Loving Indifference
Leo	John	Pride; Willfulness	Humility; Love; Gentleness
Virgo	Philip	Fault-finding; Exacting	Grace; Forgiveness
Libra	Bartholomew	Equivocation; Uncertainty	Balance; Judgment
Scorpio	Thomas	Doubt; Scorn; Suspicion	Trust; Faith; Hope
Sagittarius	James	Recklessness; Foolishness	Wisdom
Capricorn	Matthew	Self-aggrandizement	Unselfishness; Purity
Aquarius	Jude (Thaddaeus]	Eccentricity; Alienation	Altruism; Brotherhood
Pisces	Judas/(Jesus)*	Materialism	Spirituality

in one of the readings:

> This building [the Great Pyramid] . . . was formed
> according to that which had been worked out by Ra
> Ta in the mount as related to the position of the
> various stars, that acted in the place about which
> this particular solar system circles in its activity, go-
> ing towards what? That same name as to which the
> priest was banished—the constellation of Libra, or
> to Libya were these people sent. 294-151

This alludes, of course, to Edgar Cayce's incarnation
in ancient Egypt as the High Priest Ra, or Ra Ta, who had
actually come to that land from the Caucasian hills, near
what is now Mount Ararat. But his priesthood in Egypt
was interrupted by a nine-year period of exile to one of
the high Nubian hills, in what is now the Sudan region
and (by name only) an extension of the Libyan Desert.
The current rulership in Libya, however, has already
once invaded the neighboring state of Chad, and appears to have a covetous eye upon the Sudan, as well.
Since our cited excerpt from reading 294-151 makes it
clear that the Nubian mount of Ra's temporary exile was
under the domain of ancient Libya at that time, we may
well be witnessing the beginnings of a cyclical return of
certain historical phases . . . At any rate, another reading—one which speaks of things to come—says: "Strifes
will arise through the period . . . Watch for them in Libya
and in Egypt . . . " (3976-26)

So much for the mundane phase of coming changes.
An enigma of a more esoteric nature confronts us with
that astrological reference to the apparent movement of
our solar system towards the constellation of Libra—
symbol of balance! Surely the correlation with Libya, a
state presently in the throes of extreme political imbal-
ance, is both implausible and puzzling.

The trouble lies in our perspective. We need a larger view, unlimited by the blinding immediacy of current events.

A time of fulfillment approaches, as foretold. A New Age begins. And history tends to repeat itself, although the cycles carry us upward in our evolution. There will be another shifting of the poles, we are told, which may greatly alter astrological foundations. What role, if any, does Libra play in all of this, if we are headed there? Do we have a rendezvous with destiny at some far-off point in time and space within that minor constellation's realm of influence? And with the acting-out of everything in cycles, as it were, is there to be some inscrutable role ahead for that land so seemingly hostile today towards the West—namely, Libya?

Cogent questions, these. The answers lie ahead of us. And they may lie, to some extent, within the realm of astrological prediction, as our "New Age" astrologers begin to grasp the marvelous workings of their art as it was apparently practiced aeons ago, by Ra and Hermes in the Nubian mount.

Meanwhile, we have some clues at hand for a working hypothesis of sorts.

In a remarkable little book that combines both scholarly and esoteric dimensions, an Anglican clergyman named E.W. Bullinger (a direct descendant of the great Bullinger of the Swiss Reformation) created quite a stir in ecclesiastical circles in the latter part of the nineteenth century with an exquisitely researched and highly original interpretation of the zodiac, viewed from a biblical perspective. His book, *The Witness of the Stars,* first published in London in 1893, began with the proposition that the true primogenitor of the zodiac was apparently at a point somewhere in the constellation of Virgo (sign of the "virgin"). By inference, if we trace the precession of the equinoxes back through the Grand Cycle of the Ages to its last "beginning," in Virgo, using an approximate measuring-stick of 2,160 years for the backward-moving passage of the precession through each of the individual "ages" along the way (starting from the cusp of the Age of Aquarius, where we now stand), we arrive at a period somewhere between 13,119 B.C. and 10,960 B.C., which is the time-span of the Age of Virgo. Somewhere within that frame of reference, according to Bullinger's interpretation of events, Adamic Man must have had his beginnings. Bullinger, however, seems scrupulously to have avoided making such a controversial inference as to the days of Adam and Eve, and the Garden of Eden, instead contenting himself with a more narrow and specialized view: the *forward* progression of the zodiacal signs in the path of the Sun's annual ecliptic, in which he was able to trace a remarkable pattern of the Redeemer's advent and history.

We shall come to that.

First, however, let us further consider the precession of the equinoxes, based upon Virgo as our ancient starting-point. Where does this lead us? Why, to a point somewhere in the Age of Libra—even as Cayce prophesied—as the terminal point for the current Grand Cycle of the Ages, covering a time-span of some 25,920 years! The Age of Libra will take place from A.D. 10,641 to A.D. 12,800. Is this age to mark the "end of time," as we know it? Will all prophecy pertaining to man's evolution and soul development within the earth plane then be fulfilled, as we take flight to other mansions? It is an interesting speculation!

Back to Bullinger . . .

His counterclockwise view of the zodiacal wheel, based on the Sun's annual passage through the twelve signs, starts with the "virgin," in Virgo, which is the prelude to the coming of a Holy "Seed," or Redeemer, and ends with the constellation of Leo (the Lion of the Tribe of Judah), symbol of His Second Coming, in glorious victory over His enemies. And Bullinger even views the Egyptian Sphinx as a representation, esoterically conceived by early astrologers, of the conjoining of Virgo and Leo. Throughout his book, Bullinger presents his case with scholarly skill and mastery, as he moves from one constellation to the next in revealing what he believes to have been an ancient teaching of things to come, prophetically given to mankind by Adam or Enoch, in the beginning, but largely corrupted and "lost" as Greek and Roman myth systems were superimposed upon the original zodiacal symbols. A linguist *par excellence*, Bullinger provides the reader with the meanings originally ascribed to various stars, asterisms, and constellations by ancient Hebrew, Egyptian, and Chaldean star-gazers, as well as probing some of the interpretations found in Sanskrit, and finally showing how the Greek and Latin corruptions—some of which retained certain aspects of the original teaching, but in a less-than-recognizable disguise—finally gave us the zodiac we know today, which, alas, is devoid of its sacred origins and meanings.

In summary, then, when we speak of a "New Age" astrology, what are we really talking about but a rebirth of the old? For, in truth, there is nothing new under the Sun.

To conclude these philosophical observations, we revert to our initial premise: the Word.

As the Master gave, "Before Abraham was I AM before the worlds were I AM." 262-57

"Before the worlds were"!
When we are attuned to Him, the Maker of the worlds, we are in touch with Eternity. And if we would but harken, we may hear the heavenly music of the spheres, which lies within us; and we ourselves are the music. Astrology merely interprets for us some of the individual

notes of that inner language through signs and symbols. As given, then:

Attune thine inner man to the harps and the chords of the universe, and harken to the love that brings service—service—to all. 1735-2

Sunspots: Signs of Turmoil

Science, albeit unwittingly, has once again corroborated psychic revelation, and this time on a most unlikely subject: sunspots.[1]

Before we examine the scientific evidence on the subject, however, let's take a look at the psychic record. At the A.R.E.'s Ninth Annual Congress, on June 21, 1940, Edgar Cayce was asked, while in a trance state, to give a discourse on sunspots, explaining their cause and effect. To any other audience, the explanation that followed would have sounded astonishing and implausible; but to the group assembled on that date, who were already accustomed to a flow of unorthodox answers and information from this same psychic channel before them, Cayce's explanation of sunspots—although undoubtedly unique, as might be expected—was neither implausible nor particularly surprising. It had a spiritual logic of its own, transcending presently accepted scientific views of man and the universe, but intuitively "right" to anyone attuned to the concepts presented in the readings. These constantly reiterate the oneness of all force. They demonstrate, over and over, our inseparable relationship with, and individual impact upon, the rest of mankind and all the world around us.

Lines of force at the unconscious level, we discover, connect all life-forms in the universe with one another, and with Spirit, which is their source, so that communications are ever possible to those "tuned in" to the universal forces. The visible universe, we are told, was created to meet the evolving needs for the soul's development upward to the Mind of the Maker, and we are reminded that "the soul of man, thy soul, encompasses *all* in this solar system or in others." (5755-2)

Consequently, it cannot come as a surprise to discover the interaction of the soul's vibration with those vibrations emanating from the various planets, or from the sun, which rules our solar system. And this, in fact, was the gist of Cayce's unconscious discourse on sunspots, in reading 5757-1, from which we quote several key passages.

First, the reading included some prefatory comments on astronomy versus astrology, which are peculiarly appropriate at this time, perhaps, when a group of leading scientists in this country has chosen to denounce astrology in a manner that has been more reactionary than objective:

Astronomy is considered a science and astrology as foolishness. Who is correct? One holds that because of the position of the earth, the sun, the planets, they are balanced one with another in some manner, some form; yet that they have nothing to do with man's life or the expanse of life, or the emotions of the physical being in the earth.

Then, why and how do the effects of the sun *so* influence other life in the earth and not affect *man's* life, man's emotions?

As the sun has been set as the ruler of this solar system, does it not appear to be reasonable that it *has* an effect upon the inhabitants of the earth, as well as upon plant and mineral life in the earth?

... For, remember, they—the sun, the moon, the planets—have their marching orders from the divine, and they move in same.

Man alone is given that birthright of free will. He alone may defy his God!

How many of you have questioned that in thine own heart, and know that thy disobedience in the earth reflects unto the heavenly hosts and thus influences that activity of God's command! For *you*—as souls and sons and daughters of God—*defy* the living God! 5757-1

As the reading proceeded, it became increasingly clear that man himself is responsible for the disruptive activities of solar storms and other phenomena resulting from sunspots, and that he has a relationship with the sun that has never been considered by modern science:

As the sun is made to shed light and heat upon God's children in the earth, it is then of that composition of which man is made, or of that termed the earth; yet, as ye have seen and know, there is solid matter, there is liquid, there is vapor. All are one in their various stages of consciousness or of activity

for what? Man—*Godly man!* Yet when these become as in defiance to that light which was com-
manded to march, to show forth the Lord's glory,
His beauty, His mercy, His hope—yea, His patience—do ye wonder then that there become reflected upon even the face of the sun those turmoils
and strifes that have been and that are the sin of
man?

Whence comest this?

All that was made was made to show to the sons,
the souls, that God *is* mindful of His children.

How do they affect man? How does a cross word
affect thee? How does anger, jealousy, hate, animos-
ity, affect thee *as* a son of God? If thou art the father
of same, oft ye cherish same. If thou art the recipi-
ent of same from others, thy brethren, how does it
affect thee? Much as that confusion which is caused
upon the earth by that which appears as a sunspot.
The disruption of communications of all natures
between men is what? Remember the story, the al-
legory if ye choose to call it such, of the tower of
Babel.

. . . These [sunspots] become, then, as the influences that would show man as to his littleness in
even entertaining hate, injustice, or that which
would make a lie.

Be honest with thyself, as ye would ask even the
ruler of thine earth—the sun—to harken to the
voice of that which created it and to give its light
irrespective of how ye act! For, as given, the sun
shineth upon the just and the unjust alike, yet it is
oft reflected in what happens to thee in thy journey
through same.

The more ye become aware of thy relationships
to the universe and those influences that control
same, the greater thy ability to help, to aid—the

greater thy ability to rely upon the God-force within; but *still* greater thy *responsibility* to thy fellow men. For, as ye do it unto the least, ye do it unto thy Maker—even as to the sun which reflects those turmoils that arise with thee; even as the earthquake, even as wars and hates, even as the influences in thy life day by day. 5757-1

Finally, in these somber words from his unconscious communion with the universal forces, Mr. Cayce gave a more precise definition of sunspots to his attentive audience, and prescribed a spiritual remedy for this solar "ailment":

Then, what are the sunspots? A natural consequence of that turmoil which the sons of God in the earth reflect upon same . . .
He has given thee a mind, a body; an earth, and land in which to dwell. He has set the sun, the moon, the planets, the stars about thee to remind thee, even as the psalmist gave, "Day unto day uttereth speech, night unto night sheweth knowledge" . . .
Know that thy mind—thy *mind*—is the builder! As what does thy soul appear? A spot, a blot upon the sun? or as that which giveth light unto those who sit in darkness, to those who cry aloud for hope? 5757-1

Now, then, let us examine sunspots through the telescope of science.

A sunspot is a broad, shallow depression lying a few hundred kilometers below the surface of the sun, and for this reason it is seen in photographs as a "black" spot. Yet that adjective is not inappropriate. A big sunspot, when it is directly facing the earth, can literally "black out" our sunlight by as much as four percent! The temperature in these spots, or depressed areas, is significantly lower than the rest of the sun, and it is widely believed that the intense magnetic fields found in association with sunspots are responsible for the reduced temperature in these depressed plains, or umbras, as they are called.

Most frequently, sunspots are found in pairs, one negatively charged and the other positive. There is generally a corresponding pair in reverse placement on the opposite side of the sun's equator, and this phenomenon suggests the passage of magnetic currents directly through the body of the sun, in response to the violent activity generated by these solar hurricanes (sunspots). Sometimes sunspots are located in bipolar clusters of varying magnitude, with the individual spots lasting from just a few days to several months; the bigger spots may be many times the size of the Pacific Ocean. By way of contrast, sunspots in the past were far less numerous than now, and sometimes appeared only singly, for a short duration.

There is a concentrated magnetic field closely allied with each spot, which appears to participate in the growth or the decay of the spot. And it is believed that the entangling of magnetic fields of opposite polarity, which virtually annihilate each other, is the cause of solar flares. The biggest sunspots are also the focal point of the largest flares, some of which rise to extraordinary heights extending for as much as 100,000 kilometers across the solar disk. These flares, in turn, are sometimes accompanied by intense bursts of solar energies, known as proton storms, affecting the earth's ionosphere. The solar wind becomes more gusty, buffeting the earth's magnetic field as it sweeps out through the solar system, and producing geomagnetic storms that disrupt communications, cause magnetic needles to vibrate, and occasionally throw power plants out of kilter. Their less visible and less immediate effects on man and the environment can only be guessed at. But consider this: Radio-astronomy has revealed the existence of ionic "noise storms," with the audible outbursts from sunspots sometimes multiplying in intensity *"by a factor of ten million in a few minutes.*[2] [Author's italics]

Science may one day conclude that the sun is a living organism. As one of the variable stars, it is pulsing regularly. There is also a pulsating rhythm to the sunspot cycles, as we shall discuss presently. In fact, Charles G. Abbot, of the Smithsonian Observatory, claims to have measured as many as sixty-four different cycles of solar fluctuation. One of these reportedly corresponds to a "212-day cycle noted in some studies of human pulse rate."[3] Others, we are told, "have been correlated with recurrent mental ailments, cholera, meningitis, gestation eclampsia, and even the suicide rate." Such findings imply a meaningful connection between man's vibrations and the sun's. We shall soon reveal yet another.

The history of sunspots can be traced to Chinese observers in the first century B.C., although those early stargazers attributed the dark spots to the passage of birds. However, in A.D. 1610, Galileo made the first scientific observation of sunspots with a telescope. Since that time, there has been a gradual accumulation of scientific data that permits a number of interesting conclusions.

Sunspot activity now occurs in paired cycles of eleven years each, with minimum and maximum phases of activity. The magnetic polarity of the spots is reversed in the second sunspot cycle, as the sun's north and south magnetic poles are exchanged. Despite its consistency, this cyclical pattern was not confirmed until 1843. Its delayed recognition was because of older records, which had shown a more erratic history of sunspot activity prior to that date. Following the discovery of sunspots in 1610, the published records initially suggested a fifteen-year periodicity; but then the number of sunspots and related solar activity declined to a very low level about 1645, remaining almost entirely absent until 1715.

"After 1715," reports Dr. E.N. Parker, in an article appearing in the September 1975 issue of *Scientific American*,[4] "the sunspot cycle as we know it today appeared and has continued ever since." Yet he cautions against "the prejudice that the eleven-year sunspot cycle with its thousands of spots in each cycle is the norm. We can only wait to see what the next few centuries bring." Parker proceeds with this further fascinating observation: "During the seventy years of inactivity observers often had to wait years to see a single sunspot, whereas now there are usually a few spots showing even during the minimum of the sunspot cycle."

Magnetic storms and auroral displays virtually disappeared during the same quiescent period. But the most intriguing aspect of that seventy-year interval when sunspots virtually ceased was the astonishing discovery, as late as 1922, that there had been an inexplicable connection between this solar phenomenon and plant growth. This discovery, reports Dr. Parker, came about rather accidentally. A.E. Douglass, whose pioneering work on tree-ring dating was first published in 1920, had noted a cyclical variation in the annual growth rate of trees, with a tendency for the rings to increase in size through one decade, then decline in the next. (He had not yet linked this phenomenon to the eleven-year sunspot cycles, however.) But as his study progressed, and he examined samples of wood several centuries old, Douglass found a remarkable absence of the usual cyclical variation during the last half of the seventeenth century or so. The annual rings for that period were virtually uniform in width and pattern. Douglass was thoroughly baffled until, in 1922, he learned of the absence of the sunspot cycle and solar activity for the seventy-year period covering the last half of the seventeenth century, and somewhat beyond, coinciding perfectly with the uniform tree-rings he had encountered in older wood samples. His finding was officially reported to the British Astronomical Association; but, as Dr. Parker says, "Why terrestrial weather and plant growth should vary in coincidence with solar activity is a mystery that has been unresolved in the half-century since Douglass' observation." And he concludes: "The problem is difficult and racked by heated controversy, but it is too important to be ignored. The growth of plants, after all, is the basis for life on the earth."

We agree wholeheartedly with that conclusion. However, we feel that the view of science is somewhat too narrow, and we would expand upon it. Quite logically, if plant life followed a more balanced pattern of growth during the seventy years of sunspot inactivity, one should expect that animal life—including man—was similarly affected by a condition of greater equanimity and balanced behavior.

Let the zoologists look to their records. It may prove interesting. As for man, we can seek confirmation in the annals of human history. And what we seek, we shall find.

We find it quite conclusively, in fact, in a record of human warfare, which is that highly aggravated symptom of "turmoils and strifes" mentioned by Edgar Cayce in his reading on the causal factors of sunspots. He has specifically referred to "wars and hates," to "anger" and "jealousy" to "injustice, or that which maketh a lie." (5757-1) War is a manifestation of all of these unworthy qualities, under the guise of self-righteousness and national pride or honor. But the sins of man are not past finding out, and God looks to the heart and the purpose within.

During the period from 1495 B.C. to A.D. 1861, the record shows only 227 years of peace to a staggering total of 3,129 years of war! And from 1861 to the present, mankind has been engaged almost incessantly in warfare somewhere or other on this beleaguered planet of ours. But what of the seventy years from 1645 to 1715? Years of turmoil, or years of peace? That is the crucial question before us.

The Thirty Years' War, which has been termed the most horrible military episode in Western history prior to the twentieth century, was waged from 1618 to 1648. But although it did not officially terminate until the Peace of Westphalia, in 1648, peace overtures had actually begun some few years earlier, and the worst of the carnage came to an end with the conclusion of the Swedish-Danish War, in *1645—the same year, it will be noted, that marked the beginning of the seventy-year hiatus in sunspot activity.* Moreover, was it more than coincidental that astronomical observations for the *preceding* thirty years had indicated two fifteen-year cycles of sunspot turbulence? The stage for the long and bloody conflict was set with the War of the Jülich Succession, which ended in 1614. And the two fifteen-year sunspot cycles extended from 1615 to 1645. (Prior to that time, of course, there was no accumulated experience in the limited reporting of sunspots to permit any scientific conclusions about them.)

After the close of the Thirty Years' War, Europe was sick of blood. It is reported in *Collier's Encyclopedia* that "a relatively pleasant interlude in the history of war followed in Europe until the beginning of the Napoleonic wars [1790-1815]." But strife and turmoil of another nature erupted in the affairs of man considerably sooner than that. For one thing, there was the beginning of the Industrial Revolution in the 1750s, which made itself swiftly felt in the military sphere, and also in accelerated colonial expansionism and suppression. But even prior to the birth of the Industrial Revolution, there was the increasing victimization of the African coastal tribes by slave traders in the first half of the eighteenth century as the development of the Caribbean sugar plantations began to grow more lucrative. In fact, the booming plantation economy of the New World, in general, caused the world slave trade to reach colossal proportions during this period, with Spanish, Portuguese, British, French, and Dutch colonialists all engaged in this cruel and inhuman institution. Asia, too, was being systematically enslaved and plundered by the same selfish European powers. Their insatiable greed seemed to grow apace with the budding new century.

In summary, one might reasonably conclude that it was man's re-emerging injustice and cruelty on a vaster scale, rather than any single historic event, that marked a full-scale resumption of the disruptive sunspot cycles in 1715, after seventy years of relative tranquility.

It is possible that an analysis of sunspot activity from 1715 to the present, which would attempt to find a correlation between the more active periods of solar turbulence and the greater turmoils in human history, might be revealing. But such a study would be complicated by the sunspot pattern of reverse polarity every eleven years, with its alternating effects, and also by a psychological problem: strifes and turmoils have their origin in a complex pattern of attitudes and emotions, which may sometimes precede the recorded actions in human history by many months, or even years.

There will probably be no further opportunity to test our psychic theory on sunspots on a realistic basis until the turn of the century, when the Aquarian Age is ushered in, with its promise of an extended period of peace. Then, if another hiatus in sunspot activity occurs, there will be little room for scientific doubt that Cayce was absolutely right, and that sunspots are signs of strife and turmoil in the terrestrial affairs of men.

Meanwhile, we must observe, with Dr. Parker, that although we have come a long way in understanding the mysteries of the sun, we still have a long way to go. For it is the mystery of man himself that underlies our search.

Age of Glory

An Interpretation of the Seventy-Year
Sunspot Hiatus (1645-1715)

A startling bit of historical evidence has turned up that enables us to enlarge upon our previous interpretation of the seventy-year hiatus in sunspot activity, from 1645 to 1715, as reported in the preceding essay.[1] First, however, we must set the stage for our story.

According to the Cayce readings, sunspots are solar disturbances caused by strife and turmoil in the earth. Those dark-looking spots on the sun's surface are actually depressed areas, marked by violent magnetic storms and solar flare-ups that are believed to have far-reaching effects on the entire solar system and probably beyond. If the readings are correct, we may assume that sunspots are triggered by the transmission of discordant vibratory impulses in a collective human pattern. These impulses are then reflected back to us in the form of rhythmic influences generated by the eleven-year sunspot cycles. Whether the wavelike movement of the cycles, with their "peaks" and "valleys" of activity, relates to a similar pattern in human behavior is uncertain. The Cayce reading on sunspots failed to specify.[2] We posit the theory that it is more in the nature of a "thrust" effect, comparable to a giant solar pulse-beat, generated by the sun in a cumulative response to the more or less constant flow of discordant human vibrations. These vibrations are regularly building up energy that must subsequently be released as solar "storms," or sunspots. (In any given cycle, of course, the spots will manifest in greater or lesser intensity, depending upon the virulence of the disruptive vibrations, which are continually gathering into eventual "storm" areas on the surface of the sun.) The "pulsation" effect of the periodic sunspot cycles, rotating in reversely charged pairs of eleven years each, would serve to propel the discharge of surplus solar energies vigorously outward on the solar wind and into the earth's magnetic field and the fields of the outermost planets, where many of the speeding particles are "trapped" and stored. It is somewhat akin to the manner of a seed-pod dispersing its contents, which are then carried by the wind for eventual sowing at pre-selected distances. In this particular case, however, the fiery "seeds" are from an abnormal crop that can presage eventual trouble. They consist of a heavy concentration of charged solar particles—primarily protons and electrons.

Science does not yet fully understand the effect of sunspots on terrestrial life, although it is acknowledged that the alternating sunspot cycles have a significant influence upon the weather. In fact, they may even appear at first glance to be beneficial, as we shall discuss later on; but this could be a tragically deceptive conclusion. For opinion is also forming, in less orthodox scientific circles, that the sunspot cycles may adversely affect the earth's spin and play a major role in the occurrence of such catastrophes as earthquakes and floods.[3] Other suspiciously baleful effects of solar flare-ups were mentioned in our previous article. In addition, a French researcher, Michel Gauquelin, has assembled an impressive body of evidence from various scientific sources in support of the view that there is a substantive correlation between the peak periods of solar activity and the increasing incidence of such disruptive phenomena as epidemics, accidents, crime, suicides, and the pathological stimulation of the nervous system, resulting in human migrations and even wars.[4] If these data are proven to be true, it can be said that mankind is constantly witnessing in the reflected activity of sunspots an inescapable application of spiritual law: "As ye sow, so shall ye reap."

However, in the relatively limited period of man's scientific observation of sunspots, dating back to Galileo's invention of the telescope in 1610, there was an unaccountable lapse of seventy years during which sunspots virtually disappeared. Observers sometimes had to wait years to see a single sunspot. This relative absence of solar turbulence, it was discovered as belatedly as 1922, had a curious impact upon plant life in the earth, as shown in the chronicles of tree-ring dating. During those seventy years of quiescent solar behavior, the rings were remarkably uniform; they did not show the variable cycles of widening and narrowing bands, a cycle now considered "normal." From this evidence, we had theorized in our earlier article on the subject, one could expect to find a correlation in the affairs of mankind, which should reveal a similar pattern of relative harmony during the seventy-year period of scarcity of sunspots. And, indeed, we found the evidence we sought by examining a history of human warfare—the most blatant testimony of turmoil and strife in earthly affairs, although not the only indicator, of course.

The record shows that this was a period of comparative calm throughout most of the world. Small wars continued to erupt, it is true, at intermittent intervals throughout the seventy-year span in question. Yet we must consider the motivation and magnitude of those occasional conflicts in terms of earlier and later wars, comparing the degree of severity or injustice and the amount of human suffering they inflicted on the world. This is the key to understanding their karmic consequences, which underlie the significance of sunspots, according to the Cayce material on the subject. For it is seen that we live in a world of relative values. Man has not yet reached that point of development which enables him to outlaw war as a solution to his disputes and problems, although such a day will surely come. But as our moral awareness advances or recedes, so does our responsibility; and the effects of our actions on the body of mankind, and upon the planet itself, must inevitably reflect the extent to which we are deviating from or conforming to our highest ideals.

The Thirty Years' War, which had seen at least a third of the population of Germany slaughtered and had wrought havoc throughout all of Europe, terminated officially with the Peace of Westphalia in 1648. However, the last big battle ended in 1645—the precise year marking the commencement of the seventy-year lull in sunspot activity. From that time forward, with the probable exception of the Battle of Blenheim, in 1704, which cost the French rather dearly, and perhaps the fierce Cossack Rebellion of 1648, which resulted in the large-scale massacre of Polish Catholics and Jews, there were no wars of mass destruction until the dreadful carnage of the Napoleonic Era began. During this relatively tranquil and happy interlude in human affairs, the Christian civilization of the West saw the dawning of an "Age of Glory" as the Classical Era in European history began, replacing the Renaissance and the Reformation. It was an age of significant progress and stability. To the East, however, the Islamic world of the Ottoman Empire had already passed its apogee, and it continued to suffer further eclipse through internal corruption and military setbacks from abroad; while Russia, under Peter the Great, was preparing at the turn of the eighteenth century to emerge as a military power to be reckoned with. But it is quite accurate to say that, from 1645 to 1715, strife of any gravely disruptive nature was mostly notable for its absence. It was a genuine hiatus. The English Civil War had virtually ended in 1644 with the decisive Battle of Marston Moor (although peace did not become official until 1646); and history has recorded that Cromwell's Protectorate, which followed, gave England "order without despotism," thus marking the commencement of a more enlightened era as the seventy-year sunspot hiatus got under way. Similarly, a progressive "new order" was about to be introduced on the Continent with the accession of Louis XIV to the throne of France in 1643. This was a particularly important event, as we shall soon see. In Asia and Africa, the masses were still dormant; while in the New World, the European colonists were much too preoccupied with their immediate problems and opportunities to turn their heads to revolution or major intercolonial strife.

The "Age of Glory" did not last much beyond the life span of most of its key figures. Moreover, the turn of the eighteenth century saw the growing enslavement and vicious exploitation of the African and Far Eastern populations by all of the major European powers and their increasingly prosperous and greedy colonies abroad. It was this cruel and inhuman activity, we have theorized, which could conceivably have brought about the reactivation, in 1715, of the sunspot cycles as they presently appear. We now offer surprising, new historical evidence on the subject. It supports our hypothesis and simultaneously expands upon it, thereby strengthening our confirmation of the psychic interpretation of sunspots.

In addressing the 1975 session of the annual meeting of the American Geophysical Union on the subject of sunspots, John A. Eddy, of the High Altitude Observatory in Boulder, Colorado, introduced what may have been intended only as a whimsical observation. Referring to the seventy-year lull in sunspot activity, which has continued to puzzle scientists up to this day, he remarked upon the fact that the period in question—1645 to 1715—coincided almost exactly with the reign of King Louis XIV of France, from 1643 to 1715. Moreover, Louis XIV, as students of history will note with a shock of recognition, was called *le Roi Soleil*—"The Sun King." (Another odd coincidence, surely!)[5]

Can there perhaps be a connection of some sort? Is this feasible?[6] Let us see. We face the task of examining the historical record to see if the influence of this gifted seventeenth-century ruler of a major European state could conceivably have been so great as to bring about an era of relative harmony and stability in world affairs for the period of his long reign—the longest reign, incidentally, of any king in modern history.

Europe, at the time of Louis XIV's ascendancy, was the undisputed center of civilization. World leadership was in its grasp. Yet, with the tragic Thirty Years' War just drawing to a close, there was great weakness and exhaustion. Faith and virtue were at a low ebb. All of the leading European powers remained distrustful of one another.

In short, the situation bordered on chaos. The time was ripe for a strong, central figure to emerge, corresponding to the heliocentric view of the universe that was just then being introduced in Europe as a result of the combined discoveries of Copernicus and his successors, Kepler and Galileo, in what astronomers have termed the Copernican Revolution. Such a figure would be destined to lead the Christian world into an era of glorious scientific and cultural progress and expanding prosperity; and Louis XIV—"The Sun King"—was seemingly picked by the gods to fill this historic role.

Since Louis XIV was only four years old when he became king of France, his mother, Anne of Austria, acted as interim regent on his behalf. But all power was actually placed in the hands of her able minister, Cardinal Mazarin—an Italian. This remarkable man of peace performed triumphantly in his diplomatic efforts, settling international differences and solving domestic troubles with equal skill and patience. In all respects, he appears to have been the perfect forerunner of the young king, and a fitting exemplar. The relationship was a most felicitous one, suggestive of a good karmic pattern being fulfilled. Louis XIV, with appropriate patience and grace, awaited Mazarin's death, in 1661, before wielding full power. He was only twenty-two at the time, but he was more than ready for the task, having been well prepared by his mentor.

Historians have differed considerably in their assessment of Louis XIV's glorious reign. Nancy Mitford, in her colorful and well-documented biography, *The Sun King,*[7] has perhaps given us one of the most complete pictures currently available. But her focus on court personalities and petty intrigue tends to obscure the spiritual implications of Louis's rule, and we have to look elsewhere for needed facts. Fortunately, they can be pieced together from various qualified sources.

We can start, perhaps, with a psychological interpretation of the period by America's leading humanistic astrologer, Dane Rudhyar:

> Interestingly, the classical society which emerged in Europe during the late sixteenth and seventeenth centuries was modeled, unconsciously no doubt, upon the pattern of the heliocentric system: an autocratic king ruled with absolute power over a country which he theoretically owned and over a people subjected to his personal will; and he was surrounded by ministers, courtiers, and servants of various ranks reflecting his power.[8]

Further, Rudhyar explores the symbolism in "The Sun King" designation:

> A society and its culture are always based upon a set of assumptions which have a metaphysical and/or religious foundation and which find their expression in great symbols and myths . . .
> We should not forget that the new mentality which took form during the Renaissance and became set during the second half of the European seventeenth century was given its basic form by astronomers who were studying the sky. European man then applied the concept of the universe as a machine to his behavior, and found in a central, all-power-dispensing Sun the symbolic justification of the divine right of kings—*le Roi Soleil.*[9]

Next, we come to the astrological record for the period. It holds a stunning surprise.

In 1650, there occurred a rare conjunction of two of the slower-moving planets, Uranus and Neptune. It lasted through 1653, although its orb of influence extended into the years adjoining both its approach and its departure. This conjunction, which takes place about every 171 years, had been making its measured and somewhat erratic approach (due to a period of retrograde motion) when Louis XIV was born; and Sakoian and Acker report that the conjunction "corresponds to a period of major spiritual and scientific progress,"[10] with many highly developed souls incarnating into the earth to further man's evolution. These souls have a high sense of social responsibility and justice; and if other planetary aspects are favorable, they are called upon to restore order where there was chaos.[11] In its highest expression, the conjunction is said to manifest as "the synthesis of Divine Wisdom and Divine Love."[12] On the available evidence, one might conclude that its key manifestation at that particular period was in the realm of enlightened leadership. This combined with great scientific and cultural achievements to prepare mankind for its next cycle of evolution. (Two great men of science, Sir Isaac Newton and Edmund Halley, were born at the approach and the decline of the 1650-1653 conjunction, respectively, while the Duke of Marlborough—whose star first rose under the military patronage of Louis XIV, but who later became the king's "nemesis"—was born in 1650.)

According to esoteric astrology, the fact that neither Uranus nor Neptune had yet been discovered[13] might account for the absence of any conscious expression in that age of the more revolutionary aspects normally associated with the Uranus/Neptune conjunction. The sign ruling France, however, is Leo—a sign denoting kingship. It favored the rule of Louis XIV at that particular time in history.

"The Sun King" was born on September 5, 1638—preceding the actual conjunction of Neptune and Uranus, of course, but sufficiently close as a result of other planetary aspects to be considered a "New Age" child. When he ascended the throne of France, at the age of four, Uranus was in the sign of Scorpio. Here it was in its "exaltation." It clearly marked a time of drastic change and regeneration for mankind. (Uranus, in fact, is now [1976] in the same position.) Neptune was over the cusp of the next zodiacal sign, Sagittarius, whose keynote is "wisdom." (Here it would be joined later by Uranus, following the latter's retrograde maneuver into Scorpio.) This Sagittarian placement of Neptune confers "a desire to spiritualize the larger social order."[14] Because his Sun was in Virgo, the sovereignty of the spirit was emphasized for "The Sun King." Yet Louis XIV is essentially regarded by astrologers "as a Leo type," we are told, "owing to the position of the planets in his horoscope."[15] Leo is traditionally the sign of kings and presidents, as already mentioned, and its keynote is "glory." Its ruler is the Sun.

The only subsequent occurrence of the rare conjunction between Uranus and Neptune, incidentally, was during 1821-1824. It produced a phenomenal array of talent extending into all fields of public service, philosophy and the arts. Some of the greater historical figures came in "on the orb," at the conjunction's approach. The years 1821-1824 saw the appearance of such divergent geniuses as Mendel and Pasteur, Ulysses S. Grant (military preserver of the Union) and Mary Baker Eddy. Marx and Engels preceded them by only a year or two. So, in fact, did Queen Victoria, as well as Susan B. Anthony. This raises a natural question: If the 1650-1653 conjunction of Uranus and Neptune produced a more or less "peaceful" generation, coinciding with a seventy-year lull in sunspot activity, why didn't the next conjunction, during 1821-1824, produce a similar era in both human and solar behavior?

A number of logical explanations are possible. The most likely explanation takes into account the positioning of the other planetary bodies in our solar system, as well as the sign in which Uranus and Neptune are found. The conjunction took place in the sign Capricorn, which is ruled by Saturn, but with Saturn in Aries, where it is in its "fall." (At the conjunction's approach, Saturn was in Pisces, which is regarded as a "difficult" position because this is a karmic sign.) According to modern astrology, this combination denotes a generation of people who want to effect important changes in society and initiate vital reforms, but—with Saturn in Pisces or Aries—the "timing" is not right to bring about the desired results. Although these people may initiate a new cycle of experience, they cannot reap the benefits of their actions. Thus, the superficial tranquility of the Victorian Era, which ushered in another "Age of Glory," one that seemingly bore many similarities to the reign of Louis XIV, was not sufficient to quell the wave of social unrest rising up in Europe and elsewhere. This undercurrent of strife and turmoil found its most tragic expression, perhaps, in the American Civil War. Disruptive forces remained very much a part of human affairs throughout the era, as the seeds of violent change in the social order took firm root. This would appear to have been the primary difference between the Victorian Age and the Age of Louis XIV: "The Sun King" reigned during a time of general contentment, and the social unrest that ultimately led to the French Revolution did not crystallize until well after his death.

Not too surprisingly, the next Uranus/Neptune conjunction took place during 1992-1995, as we passed over the cusp of Aquarius and entered more fully into the cycle of the Aquarian Age. Pluto, the outermost planet, was in Scorpio, and its message in this sign is said to be, "Regenerate or die!" Although Uranus and Neptune were again in Capricorn (ruled by Saturn, which has been called the "taskmaster"), the successful regeneration of both the spiritual and the social order are clearly indicated by the placement of Saturn in Aquarius, where it is co-ruler with Uranus. Uranus has been called the "awakener." Esoteric astrology suggests that this will be a period in human evolution when Uranus assumes full dominion over Aquarius, and Saturn's future rulership will be restricted to Capricorn. Its present role as the bridge between the lower and the Higher Self will have been fulfilled. The interpretation one finds in most texts on the subject is that it will mark an age of brotherhood and spiritual enlightenment, ruled by neither "kings" nor "presidents," but by individual Man himself, through his inner, spiritual awakening.

We conclude our comments on the Uranus/Neptune conjunction and return to our central subject, the period of Louis XIV. Those who might dispute the placement of "The Sun King" within the orbital influence of this conjunction would at least be obliged to concede that his seventy-two-year rule, corresponding so closely with the seventy-year lull in sunspot activity, probably embraced the entire life span of many advanced souls who were born in the precise orbit of the 1650-1653 conjunction. Thus, all of these souls shared in the glory of the era over which "The Sun King" presided, as the central light in a heaven of stellar luminaries.

Finally, some of the more scientifically oriented readers may not be prepared to accept the esoteric teachings of astrology which have just been presented here. While such teachings are, of course, relevant to this article, they are not altogether essential to our case. We have merely introduced, for those who are interested, certain astrological "evidence" to add weight to our testimony. Time will prove or disprove the scientific validity of astrological analyses and predictions. But if these predictions about the Aquarian Age are correct, we should definitely be able to anticipate the commencement of another sunspot hiatus at the 1992-1995 Uranus/Neptune conjunction. Meanwhile, let us proceed.

Some historians have assumed that Louis XIV's brilliant reign was motivated by a *personal* desire for power and glory. His posthumous appellation, "The Sun King"—actually inspired by the mask of Apollo that adorned the king's chambers at Versailles—is sometimes cited by his detractors as a symbol of his glory-seeking. But an objective analysis of Louis XIV's character, in our opinion, must find him motivated by aims nobler than personal ambition; and we find this view supported by Voltaire's outstanding admiration for France's most powerful and influential ruler. Voltaire was not the sort to admire a self-seeking despot; he admired "philosopher-kings," who advanced the cause of liberty and justice. There is ample evidence that Louis XIV was in this category, despite a number of contradictory acts that might appear to have marred that image temporarily. After all, a king—even one who is endowed by his contemporaries with "divine rights"—is only human. As the Cayce readings remind us, "It is the 'try' that is the more often counted as righteousness, and *not* the success or failure." (931-1)

Many of Louis XIV's virtues and weaknesses seem to run parallel with those of another king—an ancient Israelite, who ruled his people in much the same manner: Solomon. In fact, one is almost tempted to speculate that they might have been the same soul-entity, filling a given need for kingly qualities in two widely separate periods of history. We do not press the point, however. Let the reader draw his own conclusions.

Louis XIV was always resolute in protecting the Catholic faith from the splintering effect of dissident movements, even when his aims ran contrary to the political expediency of two of the reigning popes. Nor was it personal glory that made the Sun King aspire to become a Holy Roman Emperor—an aspiration that never materialized. Yet the aspiration undoubtedly reflected his strong allegiance to Church and God and an underlying sense of holy mission. At the same time, he was by no means a bigot. History has always referred to Louis XIV as "the most Christian king," which he undoubtedly was. It was perhaps appropriate that he sought obedience and unity as the key objectives of his rule.

Unlike his predecessors, Louis XIV built up a thoroughly personal system of government, presiding over the council and many of its committees himself, rather than delegating these duties to a chancellor. In fact, it will be remembered that this was the king who uttered those astonishing words, "L'état, c'est moi!"—*I am the State.* But was it the egoistic voice of a tyrant, or the natural utterance of a ruler of his times—a man, moreover, who seemed to be intuitively aware of his historic role and who accepted his kingly responsibilities as a duty imposed upon him by a Higher Authority? (The readings imply that no national leader, good or bad, is in a position of power except by the grace of God, whether he rules an empire or presides over a democracy.)

Under Louis XIV's rule, at any rate, departmental specialization became firmly established at the outset, and he allowed no single individual to hold a predominant position. In the eyes of the nobility, whose traditional influence on affairs of state was totally eliminated, it was a reign of "low, bourgeois government." In truth, however, the king had surrounded himself with men of enormous wisdom and genius—after Mazarin's death, Colbert and Le Brun come most prominently to mind—men who worked behind the scenes with quiet efficiency and unswerving loyalty, carrying out the king's wishes. Yet Louis XIV was a wise enough monarch to appease the frustrated aristocracy in other ways. During his reign the arts flourished as never before or since in French history. This was the age of Molière, Racine, and Saint-Simon, among many others. It is not surprising that the social life at Louis XIV's court became the center of European fashion. As a result, the French language was adopted by many of the courts in Europe, and rulers who came to his elegant palace at Versailles always left in envy, striving to emulate both his court and his castle in their own lands. Bloodlines connecting him to several of the thrones of Europe gave Louis XIV an ideal opportunity to exercise with generally excellent results his genius for international diplomacy. However, the general peace that prevailed in all of Europe during Louis XIV's reign was due in large measure to his neighbors' respect for his strong and well-disciplined army. Although he used it in a number of military engagements—primarily to enforce his long-standing claim, through marriage, to the Spanish Netherlands—the Sun King was essentially a man of peace. He simply did not have the cruel or unbalanced temperament of a conqueror or a bully. Yet he was capable of tragic misjudgments from time to time. The latter part of his reign saw the rapid depletion of the national treasury through a series of ill-conceived military ventures. The English, uniting with the Dutch and others in common fear of him, tried to bring the French king to his knees. They failed in their combined efforts, for Louis XIV's patriotic subjects rallied to the cause and beat them back. But the king was ultimately forced to the treaty table in 1713.

Based on the Cayce readings, one might reasonably expect that such belligerent activities, occurring from time to time during the seventy-year sunspot hiatus, should have triggered a renewal of solar flare-ups. Perhaps they did, on a minor scale. Astronomers of the period saw sunspots from time to time, in restricted numbers. However, the readings make it plain that our human interpretation of history and events is often obscured by our three-dimensional view of the universe. One has to seek the spiritual interpretation of history and look for the esoteric meaning of events underlying the visible record. In the divine plan of things, there may be modifying forces at work that lessen the karmic consequences of certain actions that we can see and interpret only in human terms of "strife and turmoil." Each age has its lessons to learn and its duties to fulfill. The final judgment is not ours. In any case, it is conceivable that, in an age that believed implicitly in the divine right of kings, Louis XIV acted out his role at all times with a sincere conviction that he was serving a Higher Justice. Thus, even when he was wrong, the sincerity of his conviction could have lessened the degree of his guilt in the eye of God. Essentially he remained always a bright symbol of unity and progress throughout the dazzling interlude of his long reign.

Louis XIV, like Solomon, had a passion for building. He gave France the Louvre and the Royal Library, which houses one of the greatest collections of books in the world. He also built the Paris Observatory and the Academy of Science. At Versailles he constructed a palace that became the greatest showplace on earth. Even as Solomon brought grandeur and substance to what David had only dreamed of, the king insisted that his architects at Versailles use the classic but simple residence constructed earlier by his father as the cornerstone, as it were, for his airy and sumptuous palace. Yet, quintessentially, it functioned more as a "country home" for a king whose heart was always close to the land.

An admirer of nature with a fondness for riding and hunting, the king spent much time in the surrounding woods and extensive gardens; and perhaps no one was closer to Louis XIV than the royal gardener, Le Nôtre, who would invariably embrace his king as a simple commoner whenever they met after a prolonged absence. If many men feared him—and they did—it was mainly because of the sense of power his presence generated and his uncanny ability to penetrate their thoughts. It certainly was *not* the result of kingly wrath; for it has been said that Louis XIV was "the politest of kings," and his ability to control his temper under stress was phenomenal. These traits served him well. Few men in positions of similar power have been as self-disciplined or as wise.

The king's weaker side, even as Solomon's, was women. He had a succession of mistresses. But his bastard sons were given the unparalleled honor of legitimacy, which further revealed his essentially democratic nature, although it of course infuriated the established aristocracy. At the same time, he was unendingly considerate toward his legitimate queen, the Infanta Maria-Teresa. Since it was not a "love match," and she was said to have had the mind of a child, it must have been trying at times to a man of Louis XIV's broad intelligence and regal temperament.

Firsthand accounts of the king's physical appearance, found in memoirs, unpublished diaries, and letters of the period, are surprising in their general agreement. They tend to confirm Bernini's idealized bust of him, rather than some of the less flattering portraits handed down, which show the king in periwig and accentuate his somewhat large nose. He was apparently a tall man, well formed, with dark, flowing locks and noble mien. In the physical summary given by Nancy Mitford it is reported, "All speak of his noble look and extraordinary grace; he never made an ill-considered or meaningless gesture so that he seemed like a deity. . . "[16]

On his deathbed, the king's basic humility was demonstrated in his touching words to his great-grandson, who would succeed him on the throne of France. Reviewing his own shortcomings and failures as his life ebbed away, the king cautioned the child not to copy him, but to remember his duty and his obligation to God. "See that your subjects honor *Him*," he told the solemn youngster.

With the death of the Sun King, in 1715, it would seem that the sun mourned also. It resumed its cycles of dark sunspots almost at once.

Epilogue

History is full of lessons for those who will seek them out. It is clear that the seventy-year hiatus in sunspot activity from 1645 to 1715 did not produce a new Ice Age, nor did it bring on a calamitous drought. Yet these are the currently expressed fears of many of our meteorologists and other "experts" as we approach the nadir of another sunspot cycle, when the number of spots traditionally falls to its "minimum" level.*

We do not deny that significant changes in our weather patterns around the globe can be expected if another long-term cessation of sunspots takes place. It is probably true, in fact, that there would be a general cooling of the earth's atmosphere. It reportedly happened once before in the recent past.[17] But is this necessarily "bad"? (There is alarming evidence that our planet has been *overheating* for quite some time!) And what about droughts in some of our present "agricultural belts"? The agronomists shake their heads glumly at that prospect. But even if the rainfall of the future should lessen dramatically in one area of the land, forcing a change of crops or an eventual abandonment of the soil, precipitation elsewhere will almost surely make new areas more fruitful, and do so on a *lasting* basis, in the absence of sunspot cycles. Thus, a temporary tragedy could become a long-range blessing. But the transition, admittedly, would lead to some suffering and hardship.

On the other hand, it is more likely that our modern technology will provide us with an easier solution. Man

---

*Written in 1976.

appears to be on the verge of controlling his environment, and he may soon be able to "create" his own weather. The present techniques of the "rainmakers" are admittedly primitive and often ineffectual: they range from "cloud-seeding" with silver nitrate to exotic experiments with vaporizing wax. But those who doubt the "miracles" born of scientific ingenuity mated to human necessity have only to visit Israel and see how its enterprising citizens have made the desert bloom. If the "rainmakers" fail, we can turn to the sea. It is to be hoped that one day our research efforts will lead to a less costly way to convert salt water to fresh. It will then be possible to irrigate all of the earth's dry plains and deserts while the sun shines down in benevolent splendor, producing unimagined harvests. Hunger will be unheard of and strife unnecessary. Then a true "Age of Glory" will begin.

Such should be the proper fruits of the approaching Aquarian Age, if the Cayce readings can be relied upon, for like begets like: what we sow in strife and turmoil, we reap in kind; but what is sown in a spirit of universal helpfulness and brotherhood, we may expect to reap in universal joy and abundance.

Notes

The Music of the Spheres

1. The galactic core, it is now theorized by astronomers, is a massive black hole in space that alternately accretes and excretes matter. (Ref. article, "The Central Parsec of the Galaxy," by Thomas R. Geballe; June 1979.)

2. Page 39, *Paracelsus: Selected Writings*, edited by Jolande Jacobi; Bollingen Series XXVIII, Princeton University Press, N.J., 1969.

3. *Ibid.*, p. 40.

4. Pages 3483 & 3634, *Arcana Coelestia*.

5. Ref. 945-1, confirming inclusion of Pluto as one of the spheres of consciousness. Also see 3126-1 and 900-10.

6. In his book, *Earths in the Universe*, Swedenborg describes in startling detail his out-of-body visitations to the various planets within our solar system, including a curious account of the inhabitants and other matters.

7. This raises an important philosophical question. To what extent may "forced labor" or Caesarean section disrupt the plan of a given soul-entity to use a certain channel for its re-entry into the earth? Does a different soul, perhaps, take over in such cases (at least occasionally) with resultant problems for all concerned? In the coming Aquarian Age, the emphasis should focus more and more upon "natural" childbirth, as opposed to the present "forced labor" techniques so frequently practiced by attending physicians for their own convenience.

8. See *Cosmic Influences on Human Behavior*, by Michel Gauquelin; Stein & Day, N.Y., 1973.

9. Ref. "Patterns of Solar and Planetary Influence," *The A.R.E. Journal*, May 1977 (Vol. XII, No. 3).

10. Ref. *The Hidden Laws of Earth: An Edgar Cayce Handbook*, by Juliet Brooke Ballard; A.R.E. Press, Virginia Beach, Va., 1979. (Note: The author is indebted to this excellent "source book" for many of the excerpts from the Edgar Cayce readings that appear in this article.)

11. William Morrow & Co., Inc., N.Y., 1976.

Sunspots: Signs of Turmoil

1. Author's update: In their book, *The Cycles of Heaven* (St. Martin's Press, N.Y., 1978; pp. 274-276), Playfair and Hill cite the little-known findings of a Russian scientist, Prof. Aleksandr Leonidovich Chizhevsky (1897-1964), who had noted a connection between solar and human activity as early as June 1915, when a large group of sunspots crossed the central meridian of the Sun at a time when the toughest battles of World War I were being fought. Following years of exhaustive research into present and past periods of human turmoil, or "mass

excitability," as he termed it, Chizhevsky theorized in 1926, in a strikingly similar but reverse approach to Cayce's explanation of the matter, that "the electrical energy of the Sun is the superterrestrial factor which influences historical processes." Yet—inconsistent with his theory, but not with the Cayce interpretation—Chizhevsky discovered a slight time-lag between peaks of mass excitability (or turmoil) and sunspot indices, with the former peaking first.
2. Page 158, *Music of the Spheres*, by Guy Murchie; Houghton Mifflin Co., Boston, 1961.
3. *Ibid.*
4. "The Sun," pp. 48-50.

Age of Glory: An Interpretation of the Seventy-Year Sunspot Hiatus (1645-1715)

1. "Sunspots: Signs of Turmoil." *The A.R.E. Journal.* A.R.E. Press: Virginia Beach, Virginia, January 1976, pp. 19-26.
2. See reading 5757-1.
3. See *The Jupiter Effect*, by John Gribben and Stephen Plagemann. New York; Walker & Co., 1974.
4. See *The Scientific Basis of Astrology*, New York: Stein & Day, 1969.
5. "The Time the Sun Lost Its Spots," by Charles Petit. *San Francisco Chronicle*, December 12, 1975.
6. A stunning correlation is found in the following excerpt from a collection of ancient Chinese manuscripts, compiled circa 1050 B.C. and known as the "Great law": "It is the duty of the government all the time to watch carefully the phenomena of nature, which reflect in the world of nature the order and disorder in the world of government . . . When the course of nature runs properly, it is a sign that the government is good, but when there is some disturbance in nature it is a sign that there is something wrong in the government . . . Any disturbance in the sun accuses the emperor."
7. New York: Harper & Row, 1966.
8. From the book *The Sun Is Also a Star*, by Dane Rudhyar. Copyright © 1975 by Dane Rudhyar. Reprinted by permission of the publishers, E.P. Dutton & Co., Inc., pp. 3-4.
9. *Ibid.*, pp. 4 and 10.
10. *The Astrologer's Handbook*, by Frances Sakoian and Louis S. Acker. New York; Harper & Row, 1973, p. 313.
11. See pp. 63-63, *Planets in Aspect*, by Robert Pelletier. Gloucester, Mass.: Para Research, Inc., 1974.
12. Sakoian and Acker, *op. cit.*, p. 313.
13. Uranus was discovered in 1781, Neptune in 1846.
14. Sakoian and Acker, *op. cit.*, p. 216.
15. *Astrology*, by Louis MacNeice. New York: Doubleday & Co., 1964, p. 91. Note: "The Sun King's" natal chart shows Jupiter rising on the ascendant. This alone would justify regarding him "as a Leo type." It

is a sign of kingly blessings, which was given special significance in ancient Chaldean astrology.

16. From the book *The Sun King,* by Nancy Mitford. Copyright © 1966 by Nancy Mitford. Reprinted by permission of the publishers, Harper & Row, p. 24.

17. The 420-year period from 1430 to 1850, which not only embraces the seventy-year sunspot hiatus but also a hypothetical period of solar minima from 1468 to 1516, is sometimes referred to in rather exaggerated terms as "the Little Ice Age," based on records of cold extrema and glacier advances during those four centuries of generally reduced solar activity, although the evidence is not yet conclusive.

A.R.E. PRESS

The A.R.E. Press publishes quality books, videos, and audiotapes meant to improve the quality of our readers' lives—personally, professionally, and spiritually. We hope our products support your endeavors to realize your career potential, to enhance your relationships, to improve your health, and to encourage you to make the changes necessary to live a loving, joyful, and fulfilling life.

For more information or to receive a free catalog, call

       1-800-723-1112

Or write

       A.R.E. Press
       215 67th Street
       Virginia Beach, VA 23451-2061

DISCOVER HOW THE EDGAR CAYCE MATERIAL CAN HELP YOU!

The Association for Research and Enlightenment, Inc. (A.R.E.®), was founded in 1931 by Edgar Cayce. Its international headquarters are in Virginia Beach, Virginia, where thousands of visitors come year round. Many more are helped and inspired by A.R.E.'s local activities in their own hometowns or by contact via mail (and now the Internet!) with A.R.E. headquarters.

People from all walks of life, all around the world, have discovered meaningful and life-transforming insights in the A.R.E. programs and materials, which focus on such areas as holistic health, dreams, family life, finding your best vocation, reincarnation, ESP, meditation, personal spirituality, and soul growth in small-group settings. Call us today on our toll-free number

1-800-333-4499

or

Explore our electronic visitor's center on the
INTERNET: **http://www.are-cayce.com**

We'll be happy to tell you more about how the work of the A.R.E. can help you!

A.R.E.
215 67th Street
Virginia Beach, VA 23451-2061